CREATIVE KEYBOARD MUSICIANSHIP

FUNDAMENTALS OF MUSIC AND KEYBOARD HARMONY THROUGH IMPROVISATION

JACK M. WATSON
University Professor of Creative and Performing Arts
College-Conservatory of Music
University of Cincinnati
Advisory Editor to Dodd, Mead & Company

CREATIVE KEYBOARD MUSICIANSHIP

FUNDAMENTALS OF MUSIC AND KEYBOARD HARMONY THROUGH IMPROVISATION

Ruth & Norman Lloyd

DODD, MEAD & COMPANY
New York   1975

CONTENTS

EDITOR'S
INTRODUCTION

Ruth and Norman Lloyd have developed a closely knit, yet flexible and comprehensive program of musical study that is unique in the true sense of the term. From beginning to end, *Creative Keyboard Musicianship* encourages creativity, minimizes rules, and provides concrete principles and techniques basic to the compositional process.

The elements of music are never presented as isolated abstractions to be learned and mastered for their own sake. Instead, they are always used for music making and for developing insight into the ways composers of various periods, styles, and genre have employed them. Ear training is another special feature of the book which, from the beginning, is treated analytically, centering squarely on the great variety of music literature contained in the book.

The range of musical examples includes music of the various style periods, folk music, blues, rock, and musical theater. Almost one hundred composers are represented.

Throughout the book, the authors guide and stimulate students to use music materials creatively. For example, on the first page (assuming little musical background on the part of students), they introduce the pentatonic scale and show students how to improvise melodies on the black keys. By the end of the first chapter, students are using ostinato in a variety of ways in improvising solos and duets, and they are extemporizing canons—all in the pentatonic scale. (Much of the Lloyds' teaching is done by indirection. Here, for instance, students are learning to employ the related principles of unity and economy of means.)

I cannot conceive of an undergraduate program dealing with the elements of music that *Creative Keyboard Musicianship* would not enrich. In addition, I can see it as a powerful tool for private and class teaching of piano. Its approach is ideally suited to self-instruction.

The eminent American composer, Vincent Persichetti, said after reading the manuscript: "The Lloyds have written a fresh and imaginative book on 'Music Through Free Keyboard Improvisation.' I would like to have known such a document when I was a student. Even now, I find it exciting and stimulating—my fingers itch to improvise on their material!" I have felt the same way every time I have gone through the manuscript.

Jack M. Watson

PREFACE

ABOUT IMPROVISATION

The aim of this book is to help the serious student of music in his quest toward the goal of complete musicianship. Musicianship is achieved in many ways: by playing music, by listening to good performances of music, by analyzing the literature and materials of music, by writing music, and by improvising music. Improvisation, the creation of music on the spur of the moment, can be as simple as humming a new tune or as complex as the group improvisations of jazz musicians. Improvised music is to written music as an impromptu speech is to a written essay, poem, or story.

In most music curricula improvisation has been a neglected area of study—in part, because the word "improvisation" has been confused with unrestrained and formless self-expression. Actually, improvisation is one of the most practical and disciplined forms of music making. It has had many applications for musicians throughout music history and its practice has led to new musical textures as well as to such early instrumental forms as the lute ricercare and the variation forms of the English virginalists. The great school of German organ composers, which reached its height in the works of J.S. Bach, developed toccatas, fantasias, and choral preludes out of improvisational techniques.

Many of the greatest figures in Western European music excelled as improvisers, and there are many stories testifying to the improvisational prowess of Bach, Handel, Mozart, Beethoven, Mendelssohn, and Liszt. It should be noted that all these men were composers and performers. Composers improvise constantly as they think their way through a composition. In fact, any musical composition might be said to be a series of accepted—as opposed to rejected—improvisations.

Improvisation was a normal form of music making until the middle half of the nineteenth century. Recitals often were concluded by improvisations on themes suggested by the audience. However, as technical display became the principal concern of the performer and his audience, the art of improvisation was neglected, except by organists and dance musicians.

Recently the situation has changed, and composers are once more asking performers of their music to improvise—sometimes within controlled limits and sometimes with complete freedom. Improvisation on this level calls for a highly developed degree of musicianship. It implies a command of all elements of music, just as it implies imagination and technical skill.

Improvisational techniques can be learned and should be part of every music student's earliest musical activities. Like the child who learns to speak before he learns to read or spell, the student who improvises can discover the joy of making his own music before he learns the grammar of music theory. And this joy can be a powerful incentive that impels the student to a deeper understanding of all music.

ABOUT THIS BOOK

Techniques of improvisations are presented in this book, not only to teach the skill of improvisation itself, but, through improvisation, to teach the basic tonal elements of music—that is, intervals, scales, and chords—and the uses of these elements in music composition. Throughout, the purpose of the authors has been to show the student how to DO something, rather than what NOT TO DO. Instead of rules, there are hints which, if observed, will lead the student along productive paths. The study and practice of the material in this book should give the student sufficient command of the elements of music to enable him to improvise freely in various musical styles; to make an impromptu accompaniment to a song, whose melody might or might not have been played "by ear"; to transpose; to improvise on rhythmic patterns; to block out the harmonic framework of a composition; to develop a sense of freedom at the keyboard; and, most of all, to gain a deeper understanding of the creative process as applied to music.

The emphasis in this book is on exploring and discovering—although there is optional drill work throughout. This is particularly true in Part I, which is concerned with the basic pitch elements of music. Each element is studied through a series of creative exercises that include hints and techniques for the use of the element, and the setting up of problems for each student to solve in his own way. Throughout this part, the student is expected to try every tonal element in as many ways as possible, without regard for how the results relate to any other music. Of course in the process of exploring the many ways in which music materials can be used, the student will be playing the piano and developing his keyboard facility.

It is presumed that the student will always be using his ears—not only to hear what he himself is doing, but also to hear what his fellow students are playing. Rather than sitting passively, the student who is not at the keyboard should be actively involved with concentrated aural analysis. In this sense, the book is as much concerned with ear training as it is with improvisation. So, too, is it concerned with all aspects of rhythm, and rhythmic activities appear on almost every page.

In Part I, pitch elements are considered in terms of their possibilities—that is, any combination or succession of tones is possible and permissible. Part II of the book provides a functional approach to the study of traditional harmony, with an emphasis on keyboard styles and sonorities. Like Part I, it deals with the creative aspect of improvisation, but within the probabilities or sound limits of that period in music history known as the "period of common practice" that ended with the highly chromatic music of the late nineteenth and early twentieth centuries. Since the book is not intended to provide a complete course in music theory, four-part chorale-style harmonization and the rules for chord connections that grew out of vocal writing are not emphasized.

HOW THIS BOOK CAME ABOUT

This book is intended for use by the nonpianist as well as by the pianist. Its origin goes back to a series of classes taught to dance and physical education majors at New York University many years ago. Faced at that time with the problem of devising a course in music that would give the student the greatest amount of background in the shortest amount of time, we rejected the usual music appreciation approach and plunged the student immediately into the making of music—even though the student might not know Middle C.

Over the years, this approach has been used in teaching music majors and nonmajors, pianists and nonpianists at Sarah Lawrence College and at the Juilliard School of Music. We feel very strongly that the nonpianist needs to develop keyboard musicianship at least as much as does the pianist. The player of a melody instrument, or a singer, can find no better aid to thinking harmonically than to work at the keyboard. We know from long experience that often the student with little or no pianistic facility can progress very satisfactorily in keyboard improvisation. Improvisation frees the student from the inhibition of the printed page and so encourages him to use finger and arm muscles over a wide range of keyboard activities.

A FEW "ADVICES" TO TEACHER AND STUDENT

There is no absolute rate of progress in the development of improvisational skills at the keyboard. Much depends on the experience and technical facility that the student brings to the study of improvisation, and much also depends on the student's seriousness and willingness to experiment.

It is not necessary to work through the early chapters in sequence, since learning rarely follows the exact outline of any textbook. Nor is it necessary for each student to solve every problem that is presented. Certain activities might be beyond the capabilities of some students and can be postponed or even omitted. Free discretionary choice on the part of the teacher is necessary and desirable.

As practicing improvisation involves exploring more than perfecting, it can be wasteful to stay too long on any exercise. The student often needs to be encouraged to move on to the new and, to him, untried. But there is no rule against going back over the same material several times. Even a simple problem can be treated in a variety of ways. With greater experience and skill on the part of the student, more possibilities become available to him.

There are "advices" spotted throughout the book. These focus on our most serious concerns, since they generally state important learning principles.

Our feeling is that there is no limit to the skill and knowledge that a student can achieve through the study and practice of the material in this book. In trying to make all parts of the work pertinent to music literature, we hope that the scope of the student's curiosity—and subsequently his learning and understanding—will be vastly increased.

Ruth and Norman Lloyd

CREATIVE KEYBOARD MUSICIANSHIP

FUNDAMENTALS OF MUSIC
AND KEYBOARD HARMONY
THROUGH IMPROVISATION

PART I
Introduction to Improvisation

1
IMPROVISING
ON THE BLACK KEYS
Black-Key Pentatonic Scales; Black-Key Pentatonic
Triads; Other Black-Key Chords

In these first two chapters, the student is given an introduction to improvising at the keyboard. Through the exercises provided, the student will begin to achieve a sense of freedom at the keyboard, as well as an understanding of some basic elements of improvisation.

BLACK-KEY PENTATONIC SCALES

The black keys of the piano, used in succession, form one of the simplest musical alphabets: the **pentatonic** or **five-tone scales**. These black-key pentatonic scales are easy to find on the keyboard and, by virtue of the intervals they contain, produce relatively consonant musical patterns. Any two or three tones of any scale—or all five tones, for that matter—can be played at the same time, and will produce a fairly agreeable harmonic sound. (Pentatonic scales using other than black keys, and which progress in different intervallic successions, will be discussed later in Chapter 5.)

EXERCISE 1: Finding Black-Key Pentatonic Scales

Any one of the five black keys may serve as the **tonic** or **keynote** of a pentatonic scale. The tones of the scale may be written as sharps or flats:

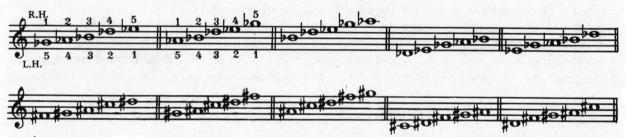

(The numbers appearing above and below the notes represent fingers. Standard piano fingering counts out from the thumb: thumb = 1; index finger = 2; middle finger = 3; etc.)

a. Accustom the fingers to the "feel" of the five pentatonic scales by playing them in all registers of the keyboard. Play them with each hand separately; with alternating hands; with both hands together. Listen to the sound of the different forms, and learn to distinguish one from another aurally.

b. Choose one pentatonic scale and, staying within its five tones, improvise a melody that is based on a short, repeated rhythmic pattern, such as in these examples:

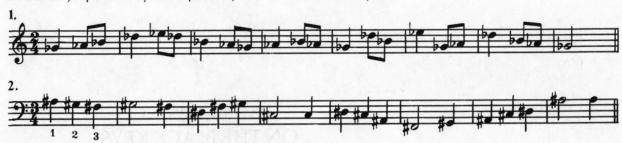

Here are some other rhythmic patterns to be used:

Be sure to improvise some melodies with the left hand and some with the right. Try the rhythmic patterns on different pentatonic scales.

c. Variety can be achieved by shifting from one pentatonic scale form to another while continuing the basic rhythmic pattern. Before shifting the keynote, play a long note. This will give time for the shift, and will provide a breathing point for the melody:

d. Improvise long pentatonic melodies based on other rhythmic patterns. Be sure to try all improvisations with each hand.

EXERCISE 2: Free Duets

Improvise "free" duets using the pentatonic scales, with one person taking the treble half of the piano, the other the bass. After agreeing on the basic pulse, or **tempo**, each player will spin out a melodic line, covering as large a segment of the keyboard as he wishes. Players can decide whether to put their melodies close together or far apart, set up rhythmic diversities such as holding one part while the other moves, and so on. The only rules are that a common pulse must be maintained, and that occasionally there must be common points of rest, or long tones, to provide a sense of cadence.

It is not necessary to refine or criticize these improvisations on the basis of musical style. They probably will not sound like Mozart—but much music doesn't. These exercises are tactile, exploratory experiments.

EXERCISE 3: Various Styles of Improvisation

Following is a series of suggestions for different types of improvisations based on pentatonic scales. Each musical example is a "starter" to be analyzed. The fragment may be continued, or the player may improvise a new idea based on the musical example. Most of the material in this and in the following exercise can be played as duets. For convenience in reading, most of the examples are written for the middle register of the piano. The student should, however, experiment in all registers and in various tempos when improvising.

*Never stop to make a correction when improvising. Always maintain an evenly flowing pulse. Think of what is **going** to happen—not of what **has** happened.*

a. Against a repeated pattern, an **ostinato**, in one hand, improvise a melody that is not too active, yet flows. Use plenty of long notes, as well as occasional ties across the bar lines. For variety, put the ostinato in the other hand. Make up ostinatos similar to that in the example and improvise on them.

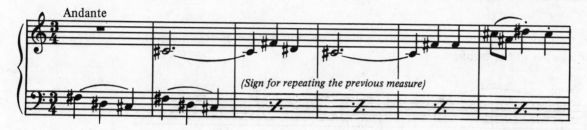

(Sign for repeating the previous measure)

b. Against a fast, repeated pattern in one hand, improvise a jagged melodic line:

c. Improvise several short pieces using melodic motion in one hand while the other hand plays a long tone on the first beat of each measure:

d. Diversify the rhythmic activity so that both parts exhibit melodic and rhythmic interest:

e. Put together combinations of two and three notes sounded simultaneously in the left-hand part:

f. Use changing combinations of two simultaneously sounding tones as accompaniments to long, singing melodies in the treble:

BLACK-KEY PENTATONIC TRIADS AND OTHER CHORDS

There are two three-tone chords known as triads within the pentatonic scales. One is on G^b (or $F^\sharp$):

The other is on E^b (or $D^\sharp$):

EXERCISE 4: Improvising with Black-Key Pentatonic Triads

Continue the ideas given below and invent others:

a. The tones of the G^b triad are played in succession as the ostinato:

b. The tones of the triad are arranged to make a waltz accompaniment:

c. Improvise extended melodies over the G^b triad; when there is a need for change, move the accompaniment to the E^b triad and continue with it until the time seems right for a return to G^b.

d. Add a second tone in the right hand under each melody tone:

e. Two-measure ostinatos may be made as follows:

f. Improvise melodies over two-measure ostinatos in 2/4, 6/8, and 4/4 time.

g. The tones of the triad can be rearranged, as in the following example, for greater resonance. Continue this example; then invent other ways in which the triads can be used in this open spacing:

EXERCISE 5: Experimenting with Other Black-Key Chords

Experiment with widespread chords that need not be triads:

EXERCISE 6: More Improvisations (Canon, Minuet, etc.)

Any scale can be used as a basis for whatever musical style a composer or improvisor wishes.

a. Improvise a simple **canon**, with the second voice imitating the first voice an octave higher or lower. Keep the rhythmic patterns as uncomplicated as possible, alternating motion and rest:

b. Improvise dance forms such as minuets, etc.:

c. Over a drum-like beat, start a melody in the tenor register and let it rise gradually to a high point and then subside:

d. Invent solos and duets (or even quartets) based on the pentatonic scale. Write the beginnings of original improvisations in notebooks as aids to memory.

EXERCISE 7: Ear Training

Ear training is an important adjunct of keyboard musicianship. Improvising depends upon the ability to hear in one's mind what is coming next. Practice in the training of the ear—in actuality, the training of the mind to be aware of what one hears—should go along with the training of the fingers. At the end of most chapters, therefore, there will be a short section referring the student to music that uses the material of the chapter, as well as a listing of melodies that are named but not quoted. The student should try from the beginning to play "by ear" melodies with which he is familiar. This experience is of great practical benefit to the student: it equips him to deal with situations where he will be expected to play without any sheet music in front of him, and it should also help him as he listens to music.

a. Play on the black keys any of the following melodies that you know. The starting tone is indicated.

1. "Deep River" (*start on B^b*)
2. "Nobody Knows the Trouble I've Seen" (*start on B^b*)
3. "Swing Low, Sweet Chariot" (B^b)
4. "The Skye Boat Song" (D^b)
5. "Auld Lang Syne" (D^b)
6. "The Farmer in the Dell" (D^b)
7. "Camptown Races" (verse only) (D^b)
8. "The Riddle Song" (D^b)
9. "Amazing Grace" (D^b)
10. "Comin' Thru the Rye" (D^b; *there will be one non-pentatonic tone*)

Find other melodies that can be played wholly or partly on the black keys.

Many American folk songs are basically pentatonic, although they might use a tone outside the scale in passing. The pentatonic scale is sometimes called the "gapped" scale because of the large intervals between B^b and D^b, and between E^b and G^b.

b. Compositions that use the pentatonic scale include the following:

1. Debussy: Préludes, Book I, No. 2, "Voiles" (second section)

2. Ravel: *Mother Goose Suite,* "Laideronette"

Find other examples in music literature.

2
IMPROVISING
ON THE WHITE KEYS
Five-Finger Patterns; Intervals; The Fifth;
Neighboring Tones; Triads

Improvising on the white keys of the piano presents new tonal possibilities. There are so many possibilities, however, that it is best to work within specific limitations. For this reason, the exercises in this chapter are based on units of five successive white keys.

Most of the musical examples in this chapter are written for the white-key unit that extends up from C to G. In practicing and improvising, the student should transfer the examples to other white-key units, noticing the distinctive sounds of the various units. The five fingers of each hand should always remain in position over the keys of the unit. When moving from one unit to another, move the whole hand, so that the fingers are positioned over the keys of the new unit as they were over the keys of the previous one:

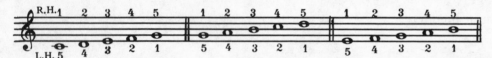

Most of these exercises can be played as solos or duets, or even trios and quartets. (Although this is primarily a keyboard book, much of the material, including this chapter, can be adapted to string, wind, and mallet percussion instruments.)

FIVE-FINGER PATTERNS

EXERCISE 1: Five-Finger-Five-Note Exercises

a. Place the thumb of the right hand on middle C, with the other four fingers falling on consecutive white keys so that the fifth finger is on the G above middle C. Move the fingers in any order, always keeping them over the same keys, and improvise short melodies that use all the white keys between C and G. Always start and end on C, E, or G. Do this in various registers, tempos, and meters.

Before starting to improvise, establish the pulse: in the arms, feet, or whole body. Let the improvisation seem to happen on top of the pulse. Rhythmic patterns have been called "surface rhythms"; they happen while the fundamental rhythm, the pulse, moves steadily and inevitably.

b. Make a long melody out of each of these beginnings. The numbers over the first note indicate which finger of the right hand is to be used:

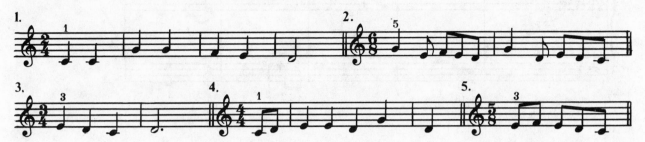

c. Place the fifth finger of the left hand on the C below middle C, with the other fingers over the adjoining white keys, so that the thumb is on the G above the C. As in the exercise above, move the fingers in any order, and improvise short melodies. Always start and end on C, E, or G.

d. Make a long melody out of each of these beginnings:

e. Familiarize yourself with the sounds made by five-key units that start on tones other than C. Use the beginnings given in the exercises above, starting, of course, on tones other than C, E, and G.

EXERCISE 2: Imitation; Contrary Motion

a. Within a five-key unit, play a two- or three-tone motive, repeating the motive in the other hand. This can be done as a solo or as a duet in which one player follows the lead of the other. An example is given below:

b. Again, as a solo or duet, play brief motives. This time, however, imitate the exact *fingering* instead of the exact *tones*. In this case, the answering voice imitates the original motive in **contrary motion**, as shown on the next page.

EXERCISE 3: Long Melodies; Cadences

Improvise long melodies that stay within a five-key unit. Before starting, decide on the basic pulse and meter to be used. Give the melodies a sense of phrase form by stopping occasionally on a long tone that suggests a breathing point or **cadence**. End on the bottom tone, or keynote of the five-key unit.

Non-final cadences, known as **semi-cadences**, should avoid the keynote. Example 1 below shows a melody with a semi-cadence on the fourth measure, and a final cadence on the eighth measure. Example 2 shows the same melody made twice as long by placing a tone other than the keynote on the eighth measure, and repeating the first six measures, this time adding a final cadence.

EXERCISE 4: Making Long Melodies out of Fragments

Make long melodies out of the fragments given below. Try them in higher and lower registers, in fast and slow tempos, and with different articulations: played in a smooth (**legato**) or detached (**staccato**) fashion. Answer a phrase in one hand with a phrase in the other, and so on.

EXERCISE 5: Arranging Melodic Series

a. In the example below, the five tones that lie between C and G have been arranged in a fifteen-tone series:

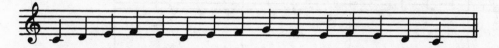

An almost limitless number of rhythmic arrangements of the fifteen-tone series can be made. Try arranging the notes in different meters; start on upbeats; introduce ties, rests, and dotted notes; use note values of varying lengths; make any other rhythmic alterations you can think of. The example below shows some of the possibilities:

Manipulate the given series of tones, playing it in at least five different arrangements.

b. Each student should write a series of twenty tones within the range of a five-white-key unit other than C–G, and dictate the series to the class. At least ten different rhythmic arrangements of these tones should be played.

c. Use the rhythmic pattern of a familiar song as the basis for a new melody in a five-key unit:

INTERVALS

An **interval** is the distance from one pitch to another. It is always measured in alphabetical terms. Intervals are numbered by counting all the different tones, or letters of the alphabet, included in the two-note span. A–E (which includes the five tones A-B-C-D-E) or C–G (C-D-E-F-G), for example, are both fifths. A–C (A-B-C) and C–E (C-D-E) are both thirds, and so on. The basic name of the interval remains constant, even when one or both of the tones has been chromatically altered with a ♮, a ♭, or a ♯. (Qualities of intervals will be discussed in detail in Chapters 3, 4, and 6.)

THE FIFTH

Combining the top and bottom tones of a five-white-key unit produces the sound of the interval of a fifth.

EXERCISE 6: The Fifth as a Drone-Bass Accompaniment

When the fifth is played regularly on an accent, it makes the accompaniment pattern known as a **drone bass**, an old musical device suggesting the bagpipe.

a. With one hand improvise a melody based on a five-key unit. With the other hand play the same fifth on the first beat of each measure, as in this example:

b. Improvise as in the example above, but reverse parts every several measures so that the right hand plays the fifth while the left hand plays the melody, as in the following example:

c. Play a fifth in the middle register of the keyboard with the left hand. Using the tones within that fifth, play a melody in the right hand that at some times is above the fifth of the left hand, and at other times below it, as in the following example:

d. Reverse the procedure, playing the fifth in the middle register with the right hand and improvising phrases that lie above and below it with the left hand.

e. Experiment with drone basses and melodies built on five-tone units other than C–G and G–D.

EXERCISE 7: Adding Motion to an Ostinato

a. Alternating or repeating tones of the drone bass makes an ostinato accompaniment which gives more motion than simply playing the fifth itself. The following examples show the beginnings of a waltz, a mazurka, and a march. Make short improvisations based on these beginnings:

b. Invent other drone-bass patterns. Then add melodies to the basses.

c. Ostinatos do not always have to be in the bass. Experiment with ostinatos in all registers.

EXERCISE 8: Combining Fifths and Using More than One Melodically and Harmonically

Long melodies seldom stay within the restricted range of five tones. The simplest way to expand the range of a melody is to move from one five-key unit to another, as in the example given below. The wavy lines indicate a certain amount of time that is spent on one unit before moving on to the next one:

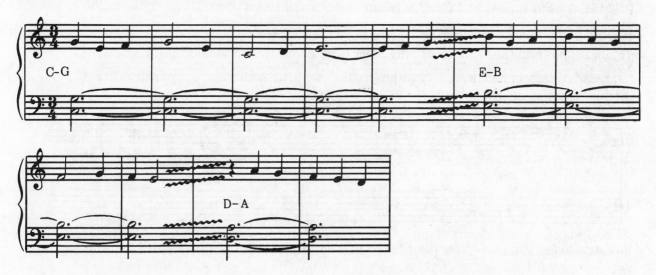

a. Improvise melodies and accompaniments that move from one fifth to another. A word of caution: *don't move from the original fifth, or a subsequent fifth, until you have worn out its sound; stay within one fifth as long as possible. Move to a new set of sounds only when your ear tells you to.*

b. Improvise short waltzes, mazurkas, folk-tune melodies, and marches that start in one unit of five tones, move to a second section based on a different five-key unit, and end by returning to the first idea and the original five-key unit. Such a three-part form whose first and third parts are more or less identical is known as a **ternary form**. The example below shows a march in this form:

Improvisation is not just a free flow of unconnected ideas. Particularly in longer melodies and forms, such as the ternary form, it is necessary to train one's memory to remember the melodic and rhythmic ideas with which an improvisation was started. Practice making mental notes about the way each improvisation begins. Notice the direction of a melodic idea, whether it moves upward or downward; note the distinctive rhythmic pattern of a motive, etc.

EXERCISE 9: Movement and Combinations of Fifths; Etudes

Up to this point in the chapter, the same interval of a fifth has been used in both hands. More interesting sounds result, however, when the tones from two fifths are combined.

a. Improvise melodies that always stay within the original fifth, with the accompanying fifth changing every so often:

b. Invent melodies that move from one fifth to another, while the accompanying fifth remains the same throughout:

c. Experiment with combinations of fifths, with each hand moving freely from one fifth to another without interrupting the rhythmic flow. Make short études based on the sound of white-key fifths, first expanding the fragments given below, and then improvising on original motives. Try various registers and spacings; play with the hands close together and far apart.

d. Combine two different fifths. In one hand play a one- or two-measure motive while the other hand plays the interval of a fifth. Move the fifths and the motive downward by step. Such a repetition of a musical idea on different pitches is called a **sequence**. Continue the following example through several sequences; invent new motives and play them in sequence:

NEIGHBORING TONES

EXERCISE 10: Use of Neighboring Tones in Melodies

The first example below shows a motive that introduces a black key within the five-white-key unit. The F♯ in the first measure functions as a **neighboring tone**, returning, as it does, to the tone it came from.

a. Invent motives that contain neighboring tones and use them in sequential patterns:

b. Try alternating a motive between the two hands:

EXERCISE 11: Neighboring Tones in Accompaniment Patterns

The neighboring-tone principle can be applied to the upper tone of a fifth in an accompaniment pattern, adding variety and more motion to the accompaniment.

a. Improvise melodies over these accompaniments and move to other fifths when a change seems called for. Note that with an active left hand there is less need for a great deal of melodic activity.

b. The example below illustrates how pattern No. 3 above can be used as an accompaniment to a blues-like tune. The typical blues progression would be: 4 measures on C, 2 measures on F, 2 on C, 2 on G, and a final 2 on C.

(Note that in jazz, the figure ♩. ♪ ♩. ♪ is often played as ♩ ♪ ♩ ♪ .)

Improvise melodies and accompaniments based on the form of the blues. You might want to add occasional black-key tones, either on or off the accent. Be sure that if you do use such tones, they move on to the nearest white key.

TRIADS

When a middle tone is added to the interval of a fifth, the result is a three-note combination known as a **triad:**

EXERCISE 12: Finding and Using White-Key Triads

a. Practice playing triads on the white keys in all registers, keeping the hands always in the same shape: the thumb and fifth finger on the outside keys, the middle tone played with the middle finger.

b. Review some of the ostinato patterns given earlier in this chapter, and improvise melodic progressions of triads over the ostinatos, as in the following examples:

EXERCISE 13: Ear Training

a. The following melodies lie within the interval of a fifth on the white keys. Play as many of them as you know. Find other melodies that limit themselves to a fifth. In the following list, the starting tone and finger of the right hand are given:

1. "Mary Had a Little Lamb" ("Merrily We Roll Along") (A-3)
2. "When the Saints Go Marching In" (C-1)
3. "Drink to Me Only with Thine Eyes" (verse only) (B-3)
4. "Home, Sweet Home" (first phrase only) (C-1)
5. "Go Tell Aunt Sally" ("Go Tell Aunt Rhody") (E-3)
6. "Shall We Gather at the River" (verse only) (E-3)
7. "What Now My Love" ("Et maintenant") (first part only) (G-1)

b. Many compositions use motives that stay within a five-key unit. As you listen to the following works, be aware of five-key groupings and try to reproduce these motives on the white keys. (The original versions are not necessarily written on white-key pitches.)

1. Beethoven: Symphony No. 9, theme of the choral finale (E-3)
2. Stravinsky: *Firebird* Suite, "Berceuse" (G-5)
3. Tchaikovsky: Symphony No. 4, last movement (E-5)

c. To see how a composer can make interesting works whose range stays within the interval of a fifth, see Bartók's *Mikrokosmos*, Book I.

PART II
Intervals, Scales,
and Chords

INTRODUCTION

Freedom at the keyboard and musical understanding depend upon knowledge and mastery of certain fundamentals of music. In the first two chapters, the student was encouraged to explore the keyboard, discovering at the same time some of the ways in which music can be made. While some technical material was included, this aspect of the study was secondary to the pleasure of actually making up melodies and accompaniments, and manipulating musical materials. It is to be hoped that the student has also learned that improvisation is not something mysterious, and that the ability to improvise lies within anyone's power.

This next unit of the book aims to further the student's explorations in music while concentrating on the elements of melody and harmony. The primary approach, again, is through improvisation. Here, however, technical drills are added. In a sense, this unit is central to mastery of the keyboard. The student who is able to perform most of the material acceptably should have no difficulties when he goes on to traditional harmony, stylistic analysis, and score reading. He will have mastered the molecules and atoms from which most music has been built.

It should be noted that, as in the first part of the book, no attempt is made to limit improvisation to any one style period. Do not try to make music that sounds like Bach or Mozart, or Bartók or Stravinsky. Let the material and the musical ideas determine the sound.

3

MINOR SECONDS
Tone Clusters; Neighboring Tones;
The Chromatic Scale

The minor **second**, or **half step**, is the smallest interval that can be played on the keyboard. It is made by playing two adjacent keys. In all but two cases, this involves a white key and a black key; the exceptions are the two white-key half steps B–C and E–F.

EXERCISE 1: Using the Minor Second Harmonically and Melodically

a. Practice playing minor seconds at random all over the keyboard, alternating hands and crossing hands over each other, as in the examples below. When covering large distances on the keyboard, choose a slower tempo than when using a smaller range. The first example below illustrates minor seconds used harmonically—played together. The second example shows minor seconds used melodically—one note after the other.

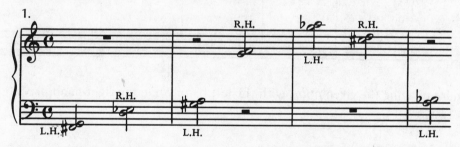

b. Play minor seconds harmonically at random. Use the following rhythmic patterns as starters, and continue each in its own spirit:

c. Play minor seconds at random melodically, using the following rhythmic patterns. Continue each pattern in a logical manner:

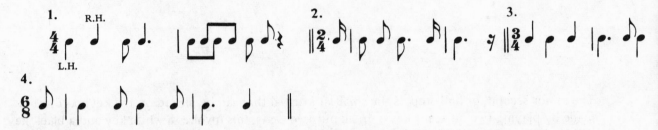

d. Play mixtures of melodic and harmonic minor seconds, using various rhythmic arrangements. Note the effect of lower and higher registers.

e. Play the notes of the example below with the right hand. Follow each note with the tone which is a minor second *below* it, played by the left hand as indicated:

f. Reverse the procedure, playing the given notes with the left hand while the right hand plays the minor second *above* each note.

EXERCISE 2: Improvisations: Ostinato, Unison, etc.

Improvise continuations of the following melodies and accompaniments. All the examples below are based on minor seconds.

a. A minor second used as an ostinato accompaniment to a melody which stresses minor seconds. Note the large intervals when the melody moves from one minor second to another:

b. Experiment with two hands in unison; then play the triplet figure with one hand and the long note with the other:

c. Here a slow duet could build to a climax in a higher register:

d. A melodic ostinato in the right hand calls for a slow-moving melody in the left hand:

TONE CLUSTERS

Adjacent minor seconds can be combined to form **tone clusters**. In the lower registers they can have the effect of drums; in the top register they can suggest bells. The examples below show, in each case, a tone cluster used as an harmonic ostinato in one hand, against which the other hand plays a melody based on minor seconds.

EXERCISE 3: Improvising with Tone Clusters

a. Continue the examples on the next page, moving the ostinatos to different pitches when variety seems called for.

b. Experiment with original improvisations using tone clusters, including those with more than three tones. Try the effect of tone clusters in the middle register, as well as in the high and low registers.

EXERCISE 4: Upper and Lower Neighboring Tones as Decoration

Minor seconds may be used as upper and lower neighboring tones to decorate a melody:

a. Play tones at random on the keyboard, and decorate each tone with neighboring tones, as in the examples above.

b. Decorate each tone of the following melodic series with its upper and lower minor-second neighboring tones:

2.

c. Play the melodic series in the examples above, omitting the principal tone at the beginning of each decorating group, as illustrated here:

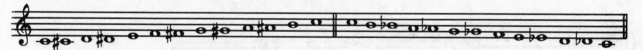

d. Play a hymn or a folk tune, and decorate each tone of the melody with upper and lower half-step neighboring tones.

THE CHROMATIC SCALE

Start on middle C, and play ascending minor seconds with the right hand until you reach the C an octave above middle C. Do the same with descending minor seconds in the left hand until you reach the C below middle C. The result in each case is a **chromatic scale**: a scale of twelve tones, each tone a minor second, or half step, distant from its neighbors. Since all intervals between adjacent chromatic scale tones are equidistant on the keyboard, the chromatic scale has no real beginning or end.

Practice playing chromatic scales ascending and descending, starting on pitches chosen at random. Use one hand at a time, or both hands together.

The ascending chromatic scale is usually written with sharps, the descending with flats:

(Key signatures may alter this procedure, as may a composer's preference, as in the Mozart example given below.)

The chromatic scale has been used, in whole or in part, primarily for decorative or coloristic purposes by many composers. In Mozart's Piano Sonata, K. 283, the following passage occurs, with the chromatic scale used to fill the gap between two D's an octave apart:

Presto

Nineteenth-century composers used the chromatic scale in glittering passage-work:

Liszt: *Gnomenreigen*

EXERCISE 5: The Chromatic Scale

a. Improvise passage-work using all or part of the chromatic scale.

b. Play chromatic scales between the melody tones of the following example. (The accompanying chords have been added to give the exercise a bit of harmonic color.)

c. Each tone of a chromatic scale can be decorated with its upper or lower neighboring tone:

1. Practice decorating each tone of an *ascending* chromatic scale with its *lower* neighbor:

2. Decorate each tone of a *descending* chromatic scale with its *upper* neighbor:

In each of the above exercises, start on various pitches, and be sure to give each hand a workout.

3. Pianists may try decorated chromatic scales in contrary motion:

d. Improvise, as duets or solos, melodic lines that wander up and down the chromatic scale in musical patterns, as in the example below. As in all improvisation, keep moving. Don't worry about dissonances that may occur in passing: by moving on, the music will ultimately come to points of resolution.

EXERCISE 6: Ear Training

a. The following melodies contain half steps which are basic thematic material. Play as many as you know; note the half steps and learn the sound of the interval by relating it to a melody you know well:

1. "I'm Dreaming of a White Christmas" (Berlin) (*start on A*)
2. "Lover" (Rodgers and Hart) (*start on C*)
3. "She Didn't Say Yes, She Didn't Say No" (Kern and Harbach) (*start on G*)
4. Bizet: *Carmen*, "Habanera" (*start on D*)
5. Fučik: *Entry of the Gladiators* (*start on C*)
6. Wagner: *Tannhäuser*, "O du mein holder Abendstern" (*start on G*)
7. Liszt: Piano Concerto No. 1 in E^b, opening (*start on E^b*).

b. Many compositions contain themes with important half steps. Here are some to look at and to listen to:

1. Wagner: *Tristan und Isolde*, Prelude
2. Wagner: *Die Walküre*, "Sleep Motive"
3. Bartók: *Music for Strings, Percussion and Celesta*, first movement
4. Bartók: String Quartet No. 4, second movement
5. Chopin: Étude in A minor, Opus 10, No. 2
6. Debussy: Études, Volume II, No. 7
7. Bartók: *Mikrokosmos*, Volume VI, Nos. 142 and 144

4

MAJOR SECONDS
AND MAJOR THIRDS
**The Whole-Tone Scale; The Major Tenth; The Tritone;
Augmented Triads**

THE MAJOR SECOND

The **major second**, or **whole step**, is equal in size to two minor seconds. It is the distance from one white key to its neighboring white key, with a black key between, as C-D. It is also the distance from one black key to its neighboring black key, with one white key between, as C#-D#. Except for the intervals E♭-F, E-F#, B♭-C, and B-C#, every major second on the keyboard consists of two white keys or two black keys. (The reason for the exceptions immediately becomes clear if you remember that B-C and E-F on the keyboard are adjoining white keys, with no black key between. These two pairs of white keys are only a *minor* second, or half step, apart.)

EXERCISE 1: Finding the Major Second

a. Practice playing major seconds at random all over the keyboard, harmonically and melodically. Alternate the hands, crossing them as necessary, as shown in the following example:

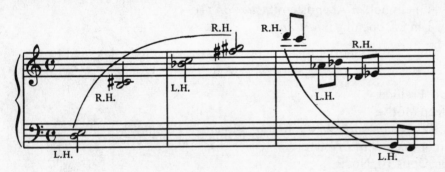

b. Play random major seconds melodically, using alternate hands, in the following repeated rhythmic patterns:

Invent other rhythmic patterns and play them.

c. Play random major seconds harmonically, using alternate hands, in these repeated rhythmic patterns:

Invent other patterns and play them.

d. With the right hand, play the series of notes given in the following example; with the left hand, follow each note with the tone that lies a major second below it, as indicated:

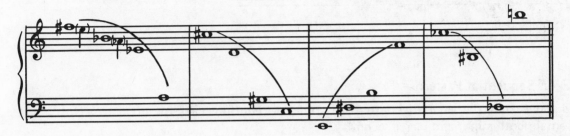

e. Reverse the procedure above: play the given notes with the left hand while the right hand plays the major second *above*.

EXERCISE 2: Repeated Major Seconds as Ostinato

A repeated major second can provide a vibrant accompaniment.

a. Continue these examples:

1. Let the right hand move up and down the white keys—always by step, never by leap:

2. Move freely by leap or step on the black keys:

b. Invent other repeated accompaniment patterns based on the major second, and improvise melodic lines over or under them.

EXERCISE 3: Decorated Chromatic Tones

a. Decorate each tone of a descending chromatic scale with its major-second upper neighbor:

b. Decorate each tone of an ascending chromatic scale with its major-second lower neighbor:

EXERCISE 4: Sequential Patterns

Analyze and play each of the sequential patterns given below; continue each for an octave. Note that some contain both minor and major seconds.

THE WHOLE-TONE SCALE

Start on middle C and play ascending consecutive major seconds until the next C is reached. Do the same, starting on C♯. Next, play *descending* consecutive major seconds starting first on middle C and then on C♯. The scale which results from playing consecutive major seconds, or whole steps, is known as the **whole-tone scale**.

There are two forms of the whole-tone scale. One form uses the three-black-key group; the other uses the two-black-key group. Any tone of either whole-tone scale may serve as the keynote. The black keys may be written as sharps or flats:

EXERCISE 5: The Whole-Tone Scale

a. Starting on G, B♭, D, A, and E, play ascending whole-tone scales covering three octaves, alternating the hands as shown:

b. Starting on D♭, F♯, B, F, and A♭, play whole-tone scales, covering three octaves, alternating the hands as shown:

c. Complete the following sequences:

EXERCISE 6: Improvisations Using the Whole-Tone Scale

a. Improvise short studies, or études, in the whole-tone scales, using major seconds, as in the example below. Change from one form of the scale to the other after a few measures.

b. Improvise short duets or solos in the whole-tone scale. Experiment with ideas that keep the hands close together; that keep the hands far apart; that use different rhythms in each hand; and so on. The following examples should be analyzed and continued. Because all tones within a whole-tone scale are equidistant, a certain monotony results if only one form of the scale is used. Change back and forth from one whole-tone scale form to the other.

THE MAJOR THIRD

The whole-tone scale contains, in addition to the major second, several other intervals that are characteristic of the scale. The **major third** is the most common of these intervals. It can be made by playing alternate tones of a whole-tone scale:

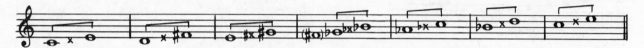

In size, the major third is equal to two major seconds:

EXERCISE 7: The Major Third

a. Practice playing major thirds at random in all registers of the keyboard.

b. Play a major third below each tone of this melody, as illustrated in the opening measure. This exercise can be played as a duet or a solo:

c. Analyze the following sequential patterns and continue each for two octaves. Practice each, one hand at a time, then with the hands together.

d. Invent additional sequential patterns that emphasize the major third and dictate them to the rest of the class.

e. Within a whole-tone scale, improvise a melody harmonized in major thirds over an ostinato, as in the fragment given below. When variety is needed, change to the other form of the whole-tone scale.

f. Over an accompaniment pattern using major thirds, improvise a melody in long note values, as shown in the example below. Change to another major third in the left hand for variety.

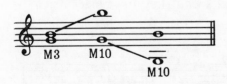

THE MAJOR TENTH

When the lower tone of a major third is dropped an octave, or the upper tone is raised an octave, the major third becomes a **major tenth**.

EXERCISE 8: The Major Tenth

a. Continue the example below, with the left hand paralleling the melody a major tenth lower, as in the first measure. Notice the satisfying resonance of this interval, particularly in the lower register of the piano.

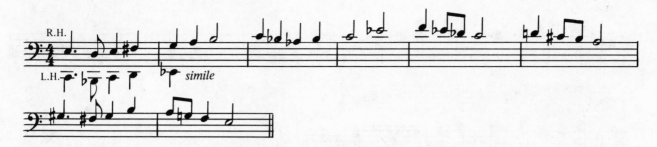

b. Play a hymn or a folk tune in the right hand. Add a major tenth below each melody tone.

c. Continue the following example. Note the use of the major tenth.

THE TRITONE

Play a keynote of any whole-tone scale, and follow it with the fourth tone of that scale:

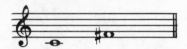

This sound, one of the most characteristic sounds of the whole-tone scale, is known as the interval of the **tritone**. Its name reflects its construction: it is made of three ("tri-") major seconds. The tritone can be written as an augmented fourth or as a diminished fifth:

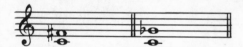

EXERCISE 9: The Tritone

a. Play tritones at random all over the keyboard.

b. Analyze the intervals of the following sequences, and continue each sequence for one octave. Note that every tritone, with the exception of the one B–F, consists of a white key and a black key.

7.

c. Continue to harmonize with a tritone each tone of the melody below. Practice the example one hand at a time; then play both hands together.

d. Play a hymn or folk tune, placing a tritone below each tone of the melody.

e. Two tritones provide an interesting harmonic ostinato. Continue the example below, in which two tritones are used as an ostinato for an improvisation in the whole-tone scale. Change from one form of the whole-tone scale to the other for the sake of variety, always adjusting the tritone ostinato to the new scale.

f. The examples below show some suggested beginnings for improvisations in the whole-tone scale featuring various uses of the tritone:

The next example is the beginning of an étude based on two tritones separated by a major third:

THE AUGMENTED TRIAD

When alternate tones of a whole-tone scale are played, the result is a three-tone chord called an **augmented triad:**

Within the augmented triad, both intervals are major thirds:

EXERCISE 10: The Augmented Triad

a. To get the "feel" of the augmented triads in the fingers, play them at random all over the keyboard. Then play a well-known tune such as "America," making each melody tone the top note of an augmented triad:

b. Continue, for a goodly amount of time, the galloping motive of the following example. Play the first tone of each triplet with the left hand, and the other tones with the right hand. Pause every now and then to allow the music to breathe. Change from one form of the whole-tone scale to the other as need for variety dictates.

c. Improvise a march, using augmented triads for a fanfare over a tritone ostinato, as in this example:

d. Make several improvisations based on the use of augmented triads. Experiment in all registers and in different tempos.

EXERCISE 11: Whole-Tone Improvisation

Any group of tones within a whole-tone scale can be sounded simultaneously.

a. Improvise short pieces based on four-tone sounds from a whole-tone scale, as in the example below. Note that the motion in the inner voices is achieved by using neighboring tones. Note also that in the spacing of the example, *the largest interval is at the bottom of the chord.*

b. Improvise pieces in the whole-tone scale alternating the motion from one hand to the other as in this example, thus creating a contrapuntal effect.

EXERCISE 12: Ear Training

a. The works of Debussy contain highly sensitive and eloquent uses of all the elements discussed in this chapter. Works containing whole-tone sections, tritones, and augmented triads are listed below. (To pinpoint the exact locations of these elements would deprive the student of the fun of discovery.)

Préludes,   Book I, No. 2, "Voiles"
                Book I, No. 6, "Des pas sur la neige"
                Book II, No. 8, "Ondine"
                Book II, No. 11, "Les tièrces alternées"
                Book II, No. 12, "Feux d'artifice"

Pour le Piano, Prélude
Images, "Cloches à travers les feuilles"
Children's Corner Suite, "The Snow Is Dancing"

b. Bartók's *Mikrokosmos* includes several short pieces based on whole-tone scales and other related material:

Mikrokosmos, Vol. III, No. 83
                  Vol. IV, No. 101
                  Vol. V, Nos. 132, 135, 136

c. Scriabin uses harmonies that are derived from the whole-tone scale, as in:

Étude in Ninths, Opus 65, No. 1 (whole-tone major ninth)
"Poème languide," Opus 52, No. 3 (whole-tone, tritone)
"Vers la Flamme," Opus 72 (tritone)

d. In Wallingford Riegger's *New and Old*, there are several whole-tone-derived little pieces:

New and Old, "The Augmented Triad"
                "The Major Second"
                "The Tritone"

5
SCALES
Major; Transposition; Modal; Natural Minor; Melodic Minor; Harmonic Minor; Unusual Scales; Key Signatures

A **scale** is a pattern of ascending or descending tones arranged consecutively in a series of intervals. Each type of scale has its own particular interval pattern, a pattern which remains the same regardless of the starting pitch. There is, for example, only *one* pattern for the major scale. But the major scale can be built on any one of the twelve chromatic tones into which the octave is divided.

Scales differ, one from another, in the number of their tones and in the arrangement of their intervals. The pentatonic scales discussed in Chapter 1 consist of five tones; the whole-tone scale is made up of six tones; and the chromatic scale contains twelve tones. In whole-tone and chromatic scales all intervals are the same: either all major seconds or all minor seconds. In the black-key pentatonic scales there are intervals of various sizes: five different interval patterns can be traced, each one dependent upon the black key which serves as the keynote.

The scales that have formed the basis of most European and American music consist of seven tones plus the octave repetition of the keynote. With one exception, the harmonic minor scale, these scales are made of different arrangements of major and minor seconds.

THE MAJOR SCALE

The **major scale** is made by playing the white keys consecutively from C up to the C above:

Minor seconds, or half steps, fall between the third and fourth and the seventh and eighth scale degrees. All the other intervals between consecutive tones are major seconds, or whole steps.

EXERCISE 1: The Major Scale

a. Play the major-scale pattern on each of the twelve tones of the chromatic C-C octave. Play the pattern at various tempos, and in rhythmic patterns such as ♩♫♩♫ and ♫♩.

Practice each scale in ascending and descending motion with each hand separately and with the hands together.

b. Play the following patterns, which call for tones of the major scale, starting each one on six different pitches:

1. 1-3-5-6-5-3-1
2. 1-5-4-3-2-1
3. 1-7-1-2-3

4. 3-4-3-2-1
5. 3-4-5-3-1
6. 3-5-3-2-1

7. 5-4-3-2-1
8. 5-6-7-8
9. 5-8-5-3-2-1

EXERCISE 2: Uses of the Major Scale in Improvisation

The major scale played in an even rhythmic pattern is not a very interesting melody. Given a bit of rhythmic variety, however, it becomes a musical idea. The examples that follow show how some composers have treated the major scale as a melody. Find other examples for yourself by looking through music.

Bach: Concerto for Two Violins

Handel: "Joy to the World"

Brahms: *Romance*, Opus 118, No. 5

Brahms: Intermezzo, Opus 117, No. 1

Chopin: Mazurka, Opus 7, No. 1

a. Improvise short compositions in the major scale by extending the examples given below. At this stage, allow melodies to move mostly by step, rather than by leap. End on 1, 3, or 5 of the scale. Analyze each fragment before improvising, noting characteristic rhythmic patterns, types of accompaniment, etc.

b. Chromatic neighboring tones can be introduced into major-scale melodies; if used sparingly, they do not destroy the key sense. Complete the following fragment and improvise other major-scale melodies that use chromatic neighboring tones:

c. Major-scale melodies often can be paralleled at the third or the tenth below the melody. The melody should begin and end on scale degree 3 or 5. Expand these beginnings and experiment with original melodies that lend themselves to this treatment:

EXERCISE 3: Emphasis on Rhythmic Patterns

A rhythmic pattern can generate a melody. The example below shows a short rhythmic pattern

♪♪ | ♩♩ which can be made into a motive that, through various forms of repetition, becomes an

eight-measure scale-line melody:

a. Improvise scale-line melodies that use the given rhythmic patterns throughout. Use a simple accompaniment that seems appropriate:

1.   Key of B♭:

2.   Key of E:

3.   Key of F:

4.   Key of D:

5.   Key of E♭:

6.   Key of G:

b. Take the rhythmic pattern of a folk song or a simple composition and improvise a new scale-line melody to fit the rhythmic pattern. The example below shows a new melody generated by the rhythmic pattern of "America":

Play each of the new melodies for the other members of the class and ask them to identify the rhythmic source.

EXERCISE 4: Transposition

The process of playing a sound that is different from the indicated written pitch is called **transposition**. There are several ways to transpose music, including the use of different clefs and harmonic analysis. For simple melodies, one of the easiest methods of transposition is in terms of scale degrees.

a. Above each note of the following C-major melodic line, write the number of its scale degree. Play the same series of scale degrees in the keys of A, B^b, G, E^b, G^b, and D. Play with hands separately and together:

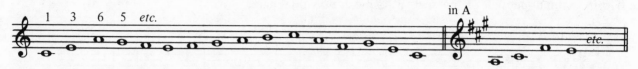

b. Write out a major-scale tune that you know; above each tone write its scale-degree number. Transpose the tune to at least five other major keys.

c. Find some simple music and transpose it to several other keys using this scale-degree method.

EXERCISE 5: Scale Degrees: The Shifting Functions of a Single Tone

Any single tone may be considered as 1, 2, 3, 4, 5, 6, or 7 of a major scale. Here is C treated this way:

Play each of the other eleven chromatic tones as 1, 2, 3, 4, 5, 6, and 7 of major scales. Be sure to play each of the scales ascending and descending.

THE MODES

Modal scales were the basic scales of music of the Middle Ages and the Renaissance. Around 1600, two of the modes—the Ionian and the Aeolian—became known as the major and minor modes, respectively, and were used almost exclusively as the basis of music until the late 1800's.

Here are the modal scales as they occur on the white keys of the piano:

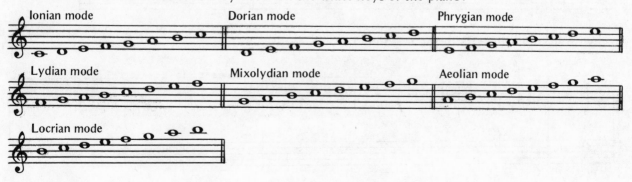

To develop a familiarity with the sound and "feel" of these modal scales, play musical "doodles" using each scale in turn. Be aware of the scale's keynote and, as in all improvisations, be sure to maintain a pulse and rhythm to keep the motion going.

The examples given below show the beginnings of melodies accompanied by simple ostinatos in each of the white-key modes. Complete the fragments, always moving from one scale-tone to the next by step except between phrases. Emphasize the most characteristic part of each scale: the tone or tones that give the mode its individuality.

a. Dorian: the upper half of this scale is its most individual part.

b. Phrygian: note the half step at the beginning of the scale.

c. Lydian: this mode sounds like the key of F major with a B♮.

d. Mixolydian: this sounds like the key of G major, except for the F♯.

e. Aeolian: this mode became the natural minor scale.

f. Locrian: note the tritone between scale degrees 1 and 5.

EXERCISE 6: Improvising in the Modes

a. Improvise original melodies with ostinato accompaniment in all the modes. Use meters of 2/4, 3/4, 4/4, 5/4, 6/8, and 9/8, in tempos that range from *adagio* (slow) to *allegro* (fast).

b. Complete the melodies and accompaniments started below:

1. Triads in the left hand move up and down over a pedal-point bass tone:

Dorian

2. The accompaniment consists of triads built on the keynote and on the tones just above and just below the keynote:

Phrygian

3. A long melody is spun over a pedal-point and two triads, the keynote triad and its neighboring triad:

Lydian

4. The right hand plays triads moving melodically by step, pausing while the left hand moves. The pattern is like a dialogue:

Aeolian

5. Two triads are used in an alternating pattern as an accompaniment:

Mixolydian

6. Triads are used melodically in the left-hand part:

Locrian

c. Improvise original short compositions using melodies and triads in the various modes.

EXERCISE 7: Transposed Modes

While the modal scales can be analyzed in terms of their whole-step and half-step structures, and while they may be built starting on any note, it is sometimes easier to think of the mode as it relates to the key of C major. In transposing a mode, it is necessary only to remember the note of the C-major scale on which the mode begins. The Dorian mode, which is the white-key scale from D to D, can be thought of as beginning on the second tone of the C-major scale. To make a Dorian scale with E as the keynote, it is necessary to find the major scale of which E is the second degree. In the case of E, that scale is D major. The Dorian scale on E would look like this:

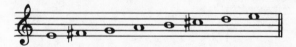

a. Play the following modal scales, ascending and descending, as review:

1. Dorian starting on C, B^b, F$\sharp$, E^b

2. Phrygian starting on B, C$\sharp$, F, D$\sharp$, G

3. Lydian starting on A^b, F$\sharp$, G, B^b, D

4. Mixolydian starting on G$\sharp$, F, E, D^b, A

5.   Aeolian starting on E^b, G$^\sharp$, B, D, F

6.   Locrian starting on A, F$^\sharp$, C$^\sharp$, G, B

b. Improvise modal music in various transposed modes and with various types of accompaniment.

INTRODUCING MINOR SCALES

Play the first five tones of the Aeolian mode beginning on A:

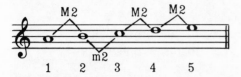

Note the minor second between scale degrees 2 and 3, and the major seconds, or whole steps, between the other adjacent tones. This five-note pattern, with the minor second between scale degrees 2 and 3, is used as the first five tones in all forms of the minor scale: the **natural minor**, the **melodic minor**, and the **harmonic minor**.

EXERCISE 8: Five-Note Minor-Scale Patterns

a. Play five-note minor-scale patterns, ascending and descending, starting on six keynotes other than the one illustrated. Be sure to use some black keys as keynotes:

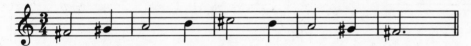

b. Select a tone. Think of it as the third scale degree of a minor scale, and play the pattern 3-4-5-4-3-2-1. Start on at least six different tones.

c. Play a tone and think of it as the fifth degree of a minor scale. Play down the scale from 5 to 1, and back up to 5. Start on at least six different tones.

d. Place the fingers of the right hand over a five-note minor-scale pattern and, over an ostinato accompaniment, improvise short melodies based on the five-note pattern. Start and end on the first, third, or fifth scale degree. Following are some suggestions which can be continued at length:

THE NATURAL MINOR SCALE

Because the intervallic relationship of scale degrees 1 through 5 is the same for all forms of the minor, it is the intervallic pattern from scale degrees 5 through 8 which distinguishes one minor-scale form from another.

The **natural minor scale** is identical with the Aeolian mode:

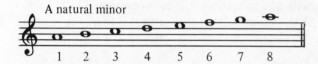

Analyze the upper part of the natural minor pattern:

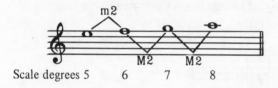

Note the minor second between scale degrees 5 and 6, and the major seconds between 6 and 7, and between 7 and 8. Thinking intervallically, play natural minor scales ascending and descending, starting on C♯, F, G, and B.

EXERCISE 9: Improvising in the Natural Minor

a. Improvise short pieces in the natural minor scale, using the beginning motives given below, as well as original ideas:

b. Spin a long melodic line in the natural minor scale over the following left-hand pattern. The pattern may be repeated as many times as necessary for the completion of the melodic idea.

c. Above each note of the American folk song, "Johnny Has Gone for a Soldier" write its scale-degree number in the key of A natural minor. Then transpose the melody to the natural minor keys of D, F$\sharp$, C, B, and E^b:

Long in the collection of John Allison who learned it from his father, who had heard it sung by a great aunt in the 1860's. Reprinted by permission of John Allison.

d. The natural minor scale shares all of its tones and its key signature with its relative major scale: that is, the major scale built on the third scale degree of the natural minor, as shown in the example below. The key signature of all forms of the minor scale is that of the natural minor. (Key signatures will be discussed in detail in Exercise 14 of this chapter.)

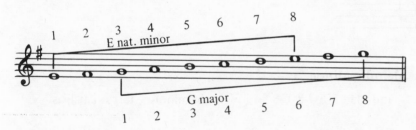

Improvise melodies that start in a natural minor key, move to the relative major key, and then return to the original natural minor.

THE MELODIC MINOR SCALE

The **melodic minor scale** is not so much an independent scale as it is a combination of other scales. It has one form when ascending, and a different form when descending:

Note that in the ascending form, scale degrees 5 through 8 form a pattern that is identical with the upper portion of the major scale:

In its descending form, the melodic minor is identical with the natural minor:

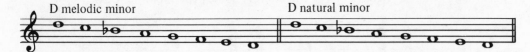

The "sensitive" tones are scale degrees 6 and 7. In general, the lowered sixth is used if the melody is coming down to scale degree 5:

If 6 moves up to 7, the raised sixth is used:

When scale degree 7 moves upward to 8, its raised form is used:

When scale degree 7 moves down, its lowered form occurs:

EXERCISE 10: Improvising in the Melodic Minor

a. Choose a tone. Call it scale degree 5, and play 5-6-7-8-7-6-5 in melodic minor. Start on at least six different pitches.

b. Play the following scale-degree patterns in at least six melodic minor scales:

1.   1-3-6-5-7-8

2.   8-7-8-7-6-5-1

3.   5-8-7-8-3-6-5-3-1

c. With the left hand, play the ascending and descending forms of the melodic minor scales on C, F, B, and E.

d. With the right hand, play ascending and descending forms of the melodic minor scales of C$^\sharp$, B^b, G and E^b.

e. Expand these beginnings of pieces in the melodic minor:

f. Make short improvisations based on the melodic minor scale.

THE HARMONIC MINOR SCALE

The **harmonic minor scale** can be thought of as a natural minor scale with its seventh scale degree raised a half step:

The characteristic intervals of the harmonic minor scale lie between scale degrees 5 and 8:

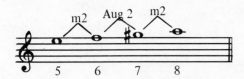

The interval between scale degrees 6 and 7 is the augmented second, an interval which is a half step larger than a major second.

EXERCISE 11: Improvising in the Harmonic Minor

a. Play scale degrees 5 through 8, first in the natural minor, then in the harmonic minor, of the minor scales of B, G, D, F♯, E♭, and C♯, as in this example:

b. In the same scales, play these scale-degree patterns, first with the left hand, then with the right:

1.   1-3-5-6-5-3-1   4.   1-5-3-1-7-1-2-3

2.   8-5-6-5-7-8   5.   1-7-1-2-3-4-5-6-5-4-3-2-1

3.   5-6-1-7-1

c. Using the rhythmic patterns $\frac{3}{4}$ ♩. ♪♫♫ and $\frac{2}{4}$ ♩ ♫♫ , play harmonic minor scales for two octaves, ascending and descending, starting on the keynotes C, F, E, B♭, and G♯. Play these scales with the hands separately; then play at least two of the scales with the hands together.

d. Above each note of the following series, write its scale-degree number in the key of B harmonic minor. Transpose the series, playing it in the keys of C, D♯, E, A, F, and G harmonic minor.

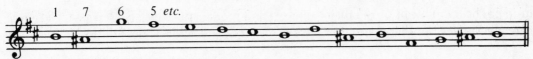

e. Transpose each of the following excerpts to at least three other harmonic minor keys. Note that in both cases the composers avoid using the augmented second melodically: they seem to think of the scale as ranging from scale-degree 7 below the keynote, to scale-degree 6 above.

1. Bach: *Two-Part Invention* No. 4

2. Handel: Sonata for Violin, Opus 1

f. Analyze the following fragments, and expand them into larger pieces:

g. Improvise short pieces that use the various forms of the minor scale. It is completely possible to use more than one form within the same piece; in fact, the use of two, or all three, forms is the rule rather than the exception. Bach seemed to be summing up minor scales in the opening of his *Chromatic Fantasy and Fugue*:

EXERCISE 12: Unusual Scales

Most familiar music has been built out of the major, minor, and modal scales discussed thus far in this chapter. There are, however, other scales that have been used, and other scales still to be explored.

a. The **pentatonic scales** based on the black keys of the piano formed the basis of the material in Chapter 1. These scales can also be formed on white keys, and on combinations of white and black keys. They can be built on scale degrees 1, 2, 3, 5, and 6 of any major scale:

    1 2 3 4 5 6   2 3 5 6 1 2   3 5 6 1 2 3   5 6 1 2 3 5   6 1 2 3 5 6

Play pentatonic scales beginning on various white keys. Improvise folk-like melodies based on these scales.

b. The Japanese use a five-tone scale that has a different structure:

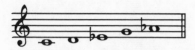

Play this scale starting on various pitches, and use it in improvisations. Try melodies played in unison, with the hands several octaves apart; also try melodies over ostinato accompaniments.

c. Some scales are classified as **"synthetic"** scales: scales that have been invented for a particular effect. Among these is the so-called "symmetrical" scale used by Rimsky-Korsakov. In this scale, minor and major seconds alternate:

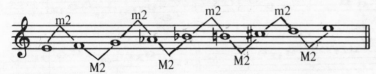

A scale might be built to cover more than an octave:

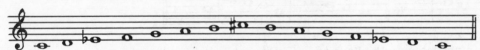

Invent two synthetic scales, and use them in improvisation.

EXERCISE 13: Reviewing Scales and Modes

a. Play the major scales of F, B, A, E^b, C♯, and A^b, ascending and descending, first with the left hand, then with the right hand. After playing each scale, follow it with its **tonic** natural **minor** (or **parallel minor**): the natural minor scale on the same keynote.

b. Play the harmonic minor scales of G, E, D, F, and B^b.

c. Play the melodic minor scales of A, E^b, F♯, A^b, and D. Start with the *descending* form of the scale, then play the ascending form.

d. Play for one octave, up and down, the following modal scales:

1. Dorian on C
2. Phrygian on A
3. Lydian on G

4. Mixolydian on F♯
5. Aeolian on B
6. Locrian on E

e. Improvise scale-line melodies based on the following rhythmic patterns:

1. In D^b major:

2. In C harmonic minor: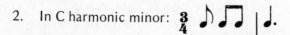

3. In B♭ natural minor:

4. In the Phrygian mode on F♯:

5. In G melodic minor:

6. In the Lydian mode on E:

f. Analyze the scale degrees involved, and continue the melodic sequences below until the next octave—above or below the starting tone—has been reached. Use the same fingering for each repetition of a unit. Then transpose the sequences to the major or minor keys of B♭, D, G, E, and A:

g. Transpose the first example below to the keys of E, G, B♭, and A major. Play the second example in the minor keys of C, D, F, and G:

h. Find several short piano pieces, similar to the ones above, which are written with a melodic voice in each hand. Transpose each piece to at least three other keys.

EXERCISE 14: Key Signatures

The arrangement of sharps or flats at the beginning of a piece of music is the **key signature**. The key signature tells the performer what key the piece of music is in; it also saves the composer the trouble of writing in every chromatic alteration, or **accidental**, in the piece: the sharps or flats in the signature are assumed to be constant throughout the piece unless otherwise indicated in the course of the music.

a. Construct major scales on the keynotes C, F, B^b, E^b, etc., continuing in this pattern of ascending fourths (or descending fifths) until C is reached again. Note that at some point enharmonic duplications will be necessary, as you move from flats to sharps. (On the keyboard, D^b major and C$^\sharp$ major duplicate each other, as do G^b major and F$^\sharp$ major, and C^b major and B major.) Write down the flats or sharps you have played for each major key:

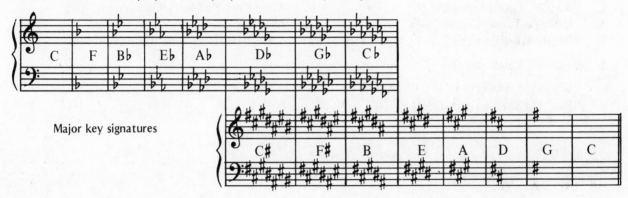

Major key signatures

b. Construct natural minor scales on the keynotes A, D, G, C, etc., continuing in a pattern of ascending fourths (or descending fifths) as above. Write down the flats or sharps you have played for each natural minor scale. You will note that these duplicate the key signatures of the major scales. The minor scales all use the key signatures of the natural minor form, which, in a sense, are borrowed from the **relative major** (the key of the third scale degree of the minor). For the melodic and harmonic minor keys, the necessary accidentals are written into the music. The pattern of minor key signatures and their relative major key signatures is:

A minor — C major	E^b minor (D$^\sharp$ minor) — G^b major (F$^\sharp$ major)
D minor — F major	A^b minor (G$^\sharp$ minor) — C^b major (B major)
G minor — B^b major	C$^\sharp$ minor — E major
C minor — E^b major	F$^\sharp$ minor — A major
F minor — A^b major	B minor — D major
B^b minor (A$^\sharp$ minor) — D^b major (C$^\sharp$ major)	E minor — G major

EXERCISE 15: Ear Training

a. In the following compositions and songs, the major or minor scale is found as an important thematic component. Pick out on the piano the tunes or themes you are familiar with. For each, the starting scale degree is given:

1. "The First Noel" (*3-2-1; then from 1-8*)
2. "Away in a Manger" ("Luther's Cradle Hymn") (*start on 5 and descend*)
3. "I Get a Kick Out of You" (Porter) (*starts on 6 and goes up to 5*)
4. "The Continental" (Porter) (*starts on 5 and goes down to 6*)
5. Tchaikovsky: *Serenade for Strings*, "Waltz" (*starts on 3*)
6. Tchaikovsky: Symphony No. 6 ("Pathetique"), third movement (*starts on 3*)
7. Haydn: Symphony No. 101 ("The Clock"), first movement (*starts on 5*)
8. Tchaikovsky: "June" (*starts on 5*)

b. The following list contains songs written in modal scales. Play by ear those tunes with which you are familiar. They do not necessarily follow the scale line. For each, the starting tone is given.

Dorian — D white-key:

1. "I Am a Poor Wayfaring Stranger" (*D*)
2. "Drunken Sailor" (*A*)
3. "Wondrous Love" (*D*)
4. "Bound for the Promised Land" (*D*)
5. "Captain Kidd" (*A*)
6. "Santy Anna" (*D*)
7. "The Sounds of Silence" (Paul Simon) (*D*)
8. "A Taste of Honey" (Marlow and Scott) (*D*)

Aeolian — A white-key, or natural minor:

1. "Willie the Weeper" (*A*)
2. "Raggle, Taggle Gypsies" (*E*)
3. "Drill Ye Tarriers, Drill" (*A*)
4. "Paddy Works on the Erie" (*A*)
5. "When Johnny Comes Marching Home" (*E*)
6. "God Rest Ye Merry Gentlemen" (*A*)
7. "We Three Kings" (*E*)
8. "Oh Come, Oh Come Emmanuel" (*A*)

Mixolydian — G white-key:

1. "Whoopee ti-yi-yo" (*G*)
2. "Rise Up Shepherd and Foller" (*G*)

6

INTERVALS
Inversion of Intervals; The Circle of Fifths;
The Diminished Seventh Chord

Intervals are the basic sounds from which melody and harmony are made. The kind of intervals a composer uses melodically influences the listener, and can make him feel that a work is highly dramatic or lyrically introspective. The harmonic use of certain intervals makes music seem tense or relaxed, emotional or bland. (Rhythm, tempo, register, and instrumentation, of course, are very important in determining the emotional quality of a musical work. But in a sense, they inflect, or intensify, the meaning of the intervals.)

Historically, the harmonic use of intervals has followed a fairly clear pattern in Western European music. Early theorists classified harmonic intervals into categories of **dissonance** and **consonance**. These classifications were based partly on the way intervals had been used, and partly on a mathematical table of ratios. Actually, the same harmonic interval can be used either as a consonance, a sound of repose, or a dissonance, an active sound, depending upon the context. (A good discussion of this subject is to be found in Vincent Persichetti's *Twentieth Century Harmony*.)

At the keyboard, it is essential to have a thorough command of all intervals. In the beginning, the student will probably have to think about each interval, and look at the keyboard as he plays it; ultimately, however, he must have an automatic sense of the size of each interval. It is important that the finger and hand muscles learn to "feel" the shape and size of each interval, and that they remember whether the interval consists only of white keys, only of black keys, or of a combination of white and black keys.

Each interval will be discussed in the following pages, with suggested improvisations and drills to give the student sufficient practice. While some of the intervals have already been introduced, they will be discussed in further detail as they appear in the traditional order of the table of consonance and dissonance, as follows:

Perfect consonance: perfect octaves, fifths and fourths
Imperfect consonance: major and minor thirds and sixths
Dissonance: major and minor seconds and sevenths; the tritone
Less usual intervals: augmented and diminished intervals

EXERCISE 1: The Perfect Octave (P8)

The **perfect octave** is the distance from one tone to the nearest identical tone above or below; for example, from any C to the C immediately above or below it:

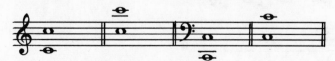

a. Accustom each hand to the "feel" of an octave by playing octaves at random all over the keyboard, one hand at a time and both hands together.

b. Improvise chant-like melodies that move stepwise and have a feeling of phrase. Play the melody in octaves in the right hand, duplicating or doubling the melody in the left hand, as in the following example:

c. Continue, for as long as seems logical, the following musical ideas based on the octave:

1. In C minor, with the tones of the octave alternating between the hands:

2. In A major, a scale-line melody in octaves over an ostinato pattern:

3. In the Phrygian mode on E, a melody consisting of repeated tones in octaves over an ostinato bass (this melody can also be tried an octave higher):

4. In a major scale and over a simple ostinato, a stepwise melody played in "broken" octaves, a favorite keyboard device of late-eighteenth- and nineteenth-century composers:

5.   Play the above right-hand patterns in the left hand, choosing a convenient register and a simple accompaniment.

d. Improvise musical ideas based on the octave.

e. Practice playing scales—major, minor, whole-tone, and pentatonic—in octaves, using the types of octave patterns illustrated.

f. Choose five melodies and play them in octaves in both hands.

g. Virtuoso pianists and composers of the nineteenth and twentieth centuries explored ways in which octaves might be used to add brilliance to their music. The following examples show a few of these. Use these patterns as the basis for improvisations:

h. Investigate the music of Liszt, Chopin, Schumann, Scriabin, Debussy, and Ravel to find other forms of octave usage useful for improvisation.

EXERCISE 2: The Perfect Fifth (P5)

The interval of the fifth was introduced in Chapter 2 as the chief form of the drone bass. It has also been the basis of most of the ostinatos used in previous chapters. The **perfect fifth** is the interval made by playing the first and fifth tones of a major or minor scale. Start on the keynote and fifth tone of C major and play an ascending chromatic scale with both hands until the C-G fifth is reached again:

Note that both tones of a perfect fifth are either on white keys or on black keys *with the exception of the perfect fifths on B^b and B,* which use one black key and one white key.

a. Play perfect fifths at random all over the keyboard until the "feel" and size of the interval is remembered by the finger and hand muscles. Usually the interval of the fifth is played with the thumb and fifth finger, but it should also be practiced with the second and fifth fingers, particularly if the bottom tone of the right hand or the upper tone of the left hand is on a black key.

In some cases, the thumb and fourth fingers will be found to be practical, as indicated in the following example:

b. Continue the following sequential patterns until the starting tone an octave higher or lower is reached:

c. Choose a melody in any scale and play it with the two hands, the left hand always playing a perfect fifth below the right hand, as in "America the Beautiful" below:

d. Improvise step-wise modal melodies harmonized with perfect fifths, with the left hand duplicating the notes of the right:

e. Continue for several phrases the following musical ideas based on perfect fifths:

1. In a black-key pentatonic scale, a long-note melody in perfect fifths over a rolling accompaniment made by combining two fifths:

2. A slow march using perfect fifths to double the melody, and accompanied by an ostinato based on two perfect fifths:

3. Under an ostinato of "violin fifths" (the tuning of the three upper strings of the violin), a folk-dance type of melody in the Dorian mode on D:

f. In the major scale, all fifths between scale degrees are perfect fifths except for the one between the seventh and fourth scale degrees:

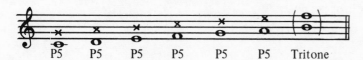

Play all the perfect fifths in the keys of F, A, E^b, B, and G major.

g. In the harmonic minor, perfect fifths occur between scale degrees 1 and 5, 4 and 8, 5 and 2, 6 and 3:

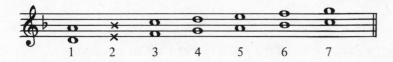

Play all the perfect fifths in the harmonic minor keys of C$^\sharp$, D, B, G, C.

h. In the natural minor, all fifths between scale degrees are perfect fifths except for the one between the second and sixth scale degrees:

Play the perfect fifths in the natural minor scales of E, F, C, B^b, and G.

INVERSION OF INTERVALS

When the top and bottom notes of an interval are reversed, the interval is **inverted**. There are several rules or principles concerning inversion of intervals:

    a. An interval and its inversion add up to nine:

       A fifth becomes a fourth; a fourth becomes a fifth.

       A third becomes a sixth; a sixth becomes a third.

       A second becomes a seventh; a seventh becomes a second.

    b. Perfect intervals remain perfect when inverted:

       A perfect fifth becomes a perfect fourth; a perfect fourth becomes a perfect fifth.

    c. Major intervals become minor when inverted; minor intervals become major:

       A major third becomes a minor sixth; a minor sixth becomes a major third.

       A minor third becomes a major sixth; a major sixth becomes a minor third.

       A major second becomes a minor seventh; a minor seventh becomes a major second.

       A minor second becomes a major seventh; a major seventh becomes a minor second.

EXERCISE 3: The Perfect Fourth (P4)

When a perfect fifth is inverted, or turned upside down, the resultant interval is a **perfect fourth**:

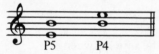

In size it is equal to two major seconds plus a minor second:

a. Play perfect fifths at random all over the keyboard, melodically and harmonically. Invert each P5 to a P4:

Note that both tones of the perfect fourth will be on black keys or white keys, except for those on F and B, where the tritone must be modified:

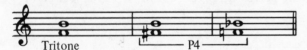

b. Continue the following sequential patterns until the starting tone is reached again, an octave higher or lower. Play first with each hand separately, then with the hands together, except for No. 5, in which the hands are divided:

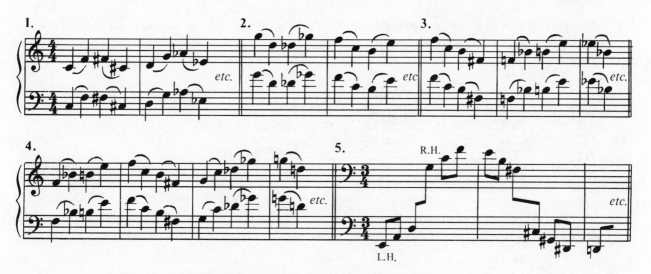

c. Play the following short melody, placing perfect fourths below each melody tone. Practice one hand at a time, then both hands together:

d. Continue the following musical motives based on the interval of a perfect fourth for several phrases:

1. The perfect fourth is used melodically in a major key over a simple ostinato or drone bass:

2. The effect of the perfect fourth is maintained even when the interval is filled in, as in the second measure of this motive:

3. The perfect fourth is sometimes used for pseudo-primitive music. Actually, it was one of the first intervals to be used harmonically. In this example, it is played over an ostinato which suggests drums:

4. The perfect fourth is featured melodically in this example, as well as providing the harmonic sound on the first beat of each measure:

5. The perfect fourth has been used as the basis for **quartal harmony**: chords built in a series of fourths. In the example below, a simple tune is harmonized with three perfect fourths below it:

e. Many twentieth-century composers, notably Schoenberg, Hindemith, Bartók, and Milhaud, show a fondness for the sound of the interval of the fourth, as illustrated by the "Sumare" from Milhaud's *Saudades do Brazil* which uses perfect fourths and tritones harmonically in both hands:

Saudades do Brazil, Vol. 2, No. 9. Max Eschig & Cie. Used by permission of Associated Music Publishers, Inc., sole selling agents.

f. Play the scale of C major, adding the **diatonic** fourth—the fourth to be found in the scale or key of C major—above each tone. The term *diatonic*, which will occur frequently later in this book, always means "within the key." Note that all the fourths are perfect, except for the one built on the fourth degree of the scale:

Tritone

1   2   3   4   5   6   7   8

g. Play all the perfect fourths in the major keys of E^b, A, F$^\sharp$, B^b, and D^b.

h. Play diatonic fourths above each scale degree in the key of A harmonic minor. Note that there are perfect fourths above scale degrees 1, 2, 3, and 5:

Tri.   Tri.

1   2   3   4   5   6   7   8

i. Play the diatonic fourths above each scale degree in D natural minor. Note that all the fourths are perfect except for the one built on the sixth scale degree:

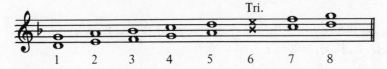

Tri.

1   2   3   4   5   6   7   8

j. Play all the perfect fourths in the harmonic and natural minor scales of G, C, B, and B^b.

k. Improvise original musical ideas using perfect fourths melodically and harmonically. Incorporate any material previously presented in this or earlier chapters.

THE CIRCLE OF FIFTHS

As its name implies, the **circle of fifths** is a series of tonal points arranged consecutively a fifth apart. When the fifths are perfect fifths, the circle will include all twelve tones of the chromatic scale:

To keep the circle of fifths within a reasonable range on the keyboard, composers often write a zigzag pattern of alternating perfect fifths and perfect fourths:

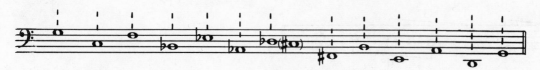

EXERCISE 4: The Circle of Fifths

a. Practice playing a circle of perfect fifths starting on B^b, F$^\sharp$, D, A^b, E.

b. Continue the following sequence. The hands start a perfect fifth apart, and progress in contrary motion. Each hand should play the circle of perfect fifths:

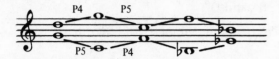

c. When a circle of fifths lies within a scale—major, minor, or modal—it moves through *seven* tones before coming back to the starting tone. In this diatonic circle of fifths, at least one of the fifths will not be perfect:

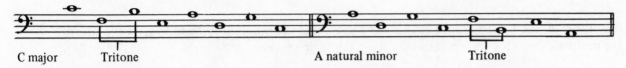

Play the diatonic circle of fifths, starting on the keynote, in the major keys of B^b, A, E, A^b, and C$^\sharp$, and in the natural minor keys of G, D, E, F, B, and C.

EXERCISE 5: The Major Third

The **major third** (M3) was introduced in Chapter 4, and will be reviewed briefly here.

a. Continue the sequence that follows, placing a major third or a major tenth over each tone of the circle of perfect fifths in the left hand:

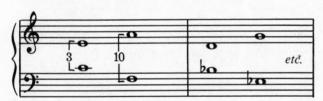

b. Analyze the following sequence, which is based on the example above, and continue it:

c. In the major scale, there are major thirds between scale degrees 1 and 3, 4 and 6, and 5 and 7:

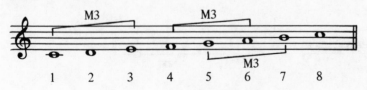

Transpose the following to the major keys of B♭, E, G, A♭, and F♯:

C: 1 - 3   4 - 6   5 - 7   8   3 - 1   6 - 4   7 - 5   8   3 - 1   4 - 6   7 - 5   1 - 3

d. In the harmonic minor scale, there are major thirds between scale degrees 3 and 5, 5 and 7, and 6 and 8:

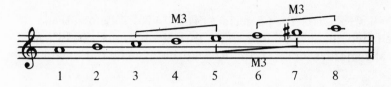

1   2   3   4   5   6   7   8

Transpose the following to the harmonic minor keys of G, B, D, F, and D♯:

3 - 5   6 - 8   7 - 5   1   5 - 3   8 - 6   7 - 5   8

e. In the natural minor scale, there are major thirds between scale degrees 3 and 5, 6 and 8, and 7 and 2:

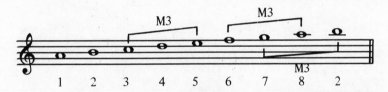

1   2   3   4   5   6   7   8   2

Transpose the following to the natural minor keys of C, B♭, E, F♯, and G♯:

A natural minor   3 - 5   6 - 8   7 - 2   8   8   2 - 7   8 - 6   5 - 3

f. Improvise short pieces that use major thirds melodically and harmonically.

EXERCISE 6: The Minor Sixth

When a major third is inverted, the resultant interval is a **minor sixth** (m6):

M3   m6   M3   m6

a. Play major thirds at random all over the keyboard, inverting each so that it becomes a minor sixth.

b. Over a circle of perfect fifths, play a major third above each bass note. Then invert the major third so it becomes a minor sixth. Continue the following sequence until C is reached again in the bass:

c. The minor sixth is a minor second, or half step, larger than a perfect fifth. In No. 1 below, the top tone of a perfect fifth is raised a half step, making a minor sixth; then the bottom tone of the perfect fifth is lowered a half step to make another minor sixth. Repeat this exercise on the indicated perfect fifths:

d. In the major scale, there are minor sixths between scale degrees 3 and 8, 6 and 4, and 7 and 5. Continue this sequence through the circle of perfect fifths:

e. In the harmonic minor scale, there are minor sixths between scale degrees 1 and 6, 5 and 3, and 7 and 5. The following example combines these and takes the sequence through the circle of fifths:

f. In the natural minor scale, there are minor sixths between scale degrees 1 and 6, 2 and 7, and 5 and 3. Continue the following sequence through the circle of perfect fifths:

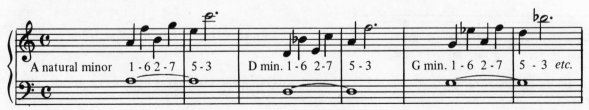

g. Analyze the following sequential patterns and continue each for one octave:

h. Improvise short musical ideas featuring the minor sixth used both harmonically and melodically. The following examples suggest some possibilities. Expand each example:

1. A simple tune moving mainly by step over an ostinato gains a certain amount of piquancy when it is duplicated a minor sixth below:

2. An ostinato composed of alternating (rocking) minor sixths in the right hand provides an interesting harmonic background to a modal melody. After a certain amount of time, the ostinato may be shifted to other tones:

3. Minor sixths can be used to good effect melodically. In this example they move up and down chromatically:

4. Minor sixths moving chromatically provide an harmonic background for a long-note melody, as in this example:

EXERCISE 7: The Minor Third

The **minor third** (m3) is equal in size to a major second plus a minor second:

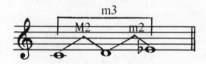

a. Play the major second C-D. Raise the top note a minor second (half step), making a minor third. Return to the major second. Lower the bottom note a minor second, making a minor third, as in the following:

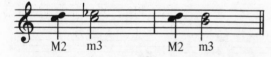

Play major seconds at random. Convert each second to minor thirds, as shown above; hands separately, then together.

b. Analyze the following sequential patterns and continue each for an octave, so that the hands get the "feel" of the minor third. Practice first with each hand separately, then with the hands together:

In this sequence, alternate minor thirds and tenths over each tone of the circle of fifths in the left hand:

c. The minor third is found between major-scale degrees 2 and 4, 3 and 5, 6 and 8, and 7 and 2:

Scale degrees 1   2   3   4   5   6   7   8   2

Transpose the following to the major keys of B♭, A♭E, C♯, and F:

1.   **2.**

D: 3 - 5   2 - 4   6 - 8   7 - 2   8   8 - 6   5 - 3   2 - 4   7 - 2   1

d. In the natural minor scale, the minor third is to be found between scale degrees 1 and 3, 2 and 4, 4 and 6, and 5 and 7:

Scale degrees   1   2   3   4   5   6   7   8

Transpose the following to the natural minor keys of B, F, C, G♯, and E♭:

1.   **2.**

1 - 3   2 - 4   4 - 6   5 - 7   8   8   7 - 5   3 - 1   6 - 4   4 - 2   1

e. In the harmonic minor scale, the minor third is to be found between scale degrees 1 and 3, 2 and 4, 4 and 6, and 7 and 2:

Scale degrees   1   2   3   4   5   6   7   8   2

Transpose the following to the harmonic minor keys of E, G, F♯, B♭, and A:

1.   **2.**

1 - 3   2 - 4   4 - 6   7 - 2   8   8   6 - 4   3 - 1   4 - 2   2 - 7   1

f. Play a familiar melody, first adding a minor third below each melody tone, then a minor third above each melody tone, as illustrated:

"London Bridge"

g. Play the following melody, adding a minor third below each tone as shown in the first measure. Practice first with the hands separately, then with the hands together:

h. A minor third becomes a minor tenth if its lower tone is dropped an octave, or its upper tone is raised an octave. Continue the right-hand part of the example below so that it is always a minor tenth above the left-hand melody:

i. Practice playing folk tunes and other melodies with one hand while the other hand plays a minor tenth above or below the melody.

j. Continue, for as long as reasonably possible, the following musical ideas based on the minor third:

1. In a minor scale, and over a two-measure ostinato, spin a melody consisting of minor thirds:

2. The motive alternates between the hands in a "nervous" rhythmic organization:

3. Running up and down the chromatic scale in minor thirds suggests Chopin's "Étude in Thirds," Opus 25, No. 6:

k. Improvise other musical ideas emphasizing the use of the minor third melodically and harmonically.

EXERCISE 8: The Diminished Seventh Chord

Starting on a tone and playing a series of minor thirds above it results in a combination of four minor thirds known as a **diminished seventh chord:**

a. Continue the following sequential patterns for two octaves:

b. Improvise in the vein of the examples below, using principally the diminished seventh chord:

c. Improvise études based on the minor third and the diminished seventh chord.

EXERCISE 9: The Major Sixth

When a minor third is inverted, the result is a **major sixth** (M6). In size, the major sixth is a major second, or whole step, larger than a perfect fifth:

a. Continue this pattern in which perfect fifths are converted into major sixths:

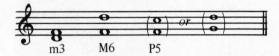

b. Continue the following sequential patterns for two octaves, always keeping the hands in the "shape" of the major sixth. It is best to practice each hand separately before playing with the hands together:

c. In the major scale, the major sixth occurs between scale degrees 1 and 6, 2 and 7, 4 and 2, and 5 and 3:

Scale degrees 1 2 3 4 5 6 7 8 2 3

Play all the major sixths in all the major keys, following the circle of fifths as in the example below:

d. In the natural minor scale, the major sixth occurs between scale degrees 3 and 8, 4 and 2, 6 and 4, and 7 and 5:

Play the major sixths in the natural minor scales in all keys, following the circle of fifths as in the example below:

e. In the harmonic minor scale, the major sixth occurs between scale degrees 2 and 7, 3 and 8, 4 and 2, and 6 and 4:

Play the major sixths in the harmonic minor scales through the circle of fifths, as in the following:

f. Improvise short musical ideas based on the major sixth used melodically or harmonically. The following examples show some of the possibilities, and should be expanded.

1. The wide spread of the tones of the major sixth is effective in a diatonic melody over an ostinato:

2. The major sixth can be combined effectively with a minor third, moving generally in the chromatic scale:

3. Major sixths moving up and down the chromatic scale over a simple ostinato suggest Chopinesque passage-work. The right-hand part of this example might be tried an octave higher than written:

4. Major sixths in the bass moving slowly down the chromatic scale provide a somewhat doleful background for a melody containing many long tones:

5. Note the use of major sixths a third apart in the next example. The G♯ of the upper voice of one sixth, followed by G♮ in the lower voice of a later sixth, creates an ambivalent effect known as a **false relation**. It has been used by composers for just this contradictory quality.

g. Play folk tunes and other melodies in one hand. With the other hand, play a major sixth above or below each melody tone. Try this in various registers.

EXERCISE 10: Combinations of Diatonic Thirds and Sixths; *Fauxbourdon*

By the fifteenth century, the intervals of thirds and sixths had become significant in Western European harmony. One of the earliest manifestations of this choice of harmonic sounds was the practice of **fauxbourdon**: the paralleling of a melody at the interval of a major or minor sixth, with a major or minor third above the bottom tone inserted, all within the key of the melody. The example below shows the beginning of "America" harmonized in this fashion:

This practice of paralleling in thirds and sixths was used by Beethoven in his Piano Sonata, Opus 2, No. 3:

a. Improvise a simple tune and parallel it with diatonic thirds and sixths in the style of **fauxbourdon**, as in this example:

b. Continue these examples, always adding a diatonic sixth below the melody tone:

  1.   A simple tune in a major scale:

2. A step-wise melody in the natural or harmonic minor:

3. A slow dance-like melody and accompaniment in the Phrygian mode:

4. An étude-like idea built on alternate thirds and sixths:

5. Alternating thirds and sixths provide a moving background for a singing melody in the left hand:

EXERCISE 11: Variation Forms Using Thirds and Sixths

a. In the simplest type of variation form, a melody and/or its bass undergo modest modifications. The example below shows a theme and variations. The theme is a scale-wise melody paralleled in thirds (tenths) in the bass. (Parallel diatonic thirds and sixths served as the basis for many variation forms in the eighteenth and nineteenth centuries.) The variations use neighboring scale tones to decorate the melody or the bass. In Nos. 2, 3, 4, and 6, the movement of the variations alternates between the hands. Complete each variation to the same length as the theme, and invent several more variations:

Theme

b. Improvise themes and variations based on major, minor, and modal scales. Each example should begin with the keynote of the scale in the left hand. The melody should move step-wise, and should be paralleled in diatonic thirds.

c. A sequential pattern consisting of alternating diatonic thirds and sixths can also serve as a theme on which to make variations. Continue the following pattern until the starting tones have been reached again, two octaves below the original tones. Note that the left hand plays the descending scale starting on the keynote of the scale. Play the pattern in three or four minor scales and modes:

Complete the following melodic variations on the pattern above, and improvise others:

Convert several of the variations above to minor.

EXERCISE 12: Combining Perfect Fifths and Fourths with Diatonic Thirds and Sixths

Composers wishing to suggest the sound of natural horns and trumpets often use a combination of sixths, perfect fifths, and thirds to harmonize the first three tones of the scale. A good example of this is in Domenico Scarlatti's Sonata in D major, L. 465 (K. 96):

Edited by R. Kirkpatrick, K96. Used by permission of G. Schirmer, Inc., sole selling agents.

a. Analyze the harmonic intervals in the Scarlatti example above. Then transpose the excerpt to the keys of B^b, F, and A.

b. Play and analyze the first four measures of the following example. Then play the pattern through the circle of fifths:

c. Repeat the exercise above in the minor scales.

d. Improvise short musical ideas based on the harmonic sounds of thirds, perfect fifths, and sixths, as above.

e. Continue each of the following patterns for two octaves. Analyze the intervals used; then practice one hand at a time before playing the patterns with the hands together:

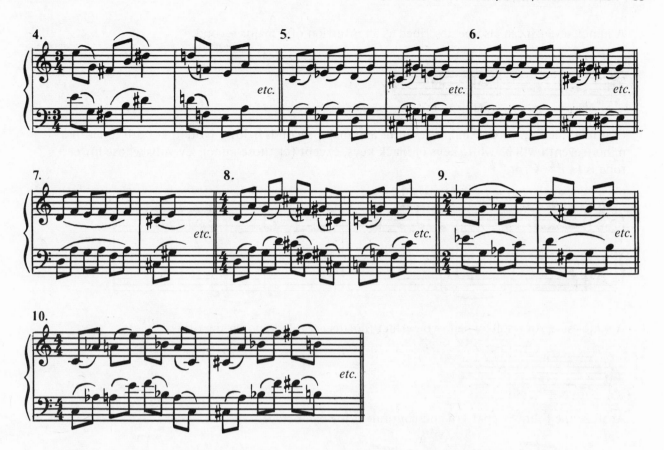

It is to be hoped that the student will concentrate on intervals aurally as well as muscularly, listening to his fellow students and becoming able to recognize right sounds from wrong ones. Also, as he listens to music, he has an opportunity to analyze mentally which intervals a composer seems to be emphasizing, or using as the basis for his music. Finally, it is expected that the student will continue to try to pick out melodies at the keyboard: simple ones at first, and more complex ones as he develops a technique of hearing.

EXERCISE 13: The Minor Seventh

The **minor seventh** (m7) is a major second smaller than an octave:

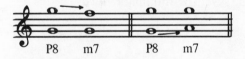

a. Analyze the following sequential patterns and continue each for an octave:

b. A minor seventh can also be described as an inversion of a major second:

Continue the sequence of minor sevenths and major seconds below. Note that both tones of a minor seventh will be white keys or black keys, except for those minor sevenths whose lower tone is F, F♯, C, or C♯:

c. A minor seventh results when two perfect fourths are piled one on the other:

Analyze the following pattern and continue it for one octave:

d. The minor seventh followed by a major third or a minor third is one of the most familiar harmonic sounds in music. Continue the examples below:

1. This pattern is taken through the circle of fifths in the left hand, while the right hand moves down the chromatic scale to make alternating harmonic minor sevenths and major thirds with the left hand:

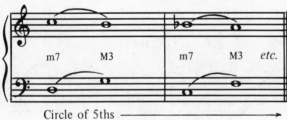

2. In this example, the minor seventh alternates with a minor third:

e. Diatonic minor sevenths can be built above all tones of the major scale except the keynote and the fourth scale degree:

1. Play all the minor sevenths in at least six major scales, following the pattern given below:

2. Improvise, over ostinato patterns, diatonic melodies that feature the minor seventh in the major scale, as in the fragment below:

f. Diatonic minor sevenths can be built above all tones of the natural minor scale except the third and sixth scale degrees. Practice playing all minor sevenths in at least six natural minor keys, using the following pattern as a model:

g. In the harmonic minor scale, diatonic minor sevenths can be built only on the second, fourth, and fifth scale degrees. Practice playing the minor sevenths in at least six harmonic minor keys, using the following pattern as a model:

h. Improvise musical ideas that feature the minor seventh both melodically and harmonically.

i. Analyze the following sequential patterns. Then play each pattern through two octaves:

EXERCISE 14: The Major Seventh

The **major seventh** (M7) is a minor second, or half step, smaller than an octave.

a. Analyze and play the following sequential patterns, continuing them until the starting tones have been reached again:

b. The major seventh is the result of inverting a minor second. Analyze the following sequential patterns, and continue each for at least one octave:

c. While the major seventh is considered one of the most dissonant of intervals, much depends on its context, the register used, and whether or not it is played percussively or gently. Improvise short musical ideas that feature the major seventh used melodically or harmonically. The following fragments should be continued for six to ten measures:

1. A simple tune in C major gains added spice when a major seventh is placed below each melody tone:

2. A strident fanfare can be based on the major seventh, mixing it with other intervals for contrast and motion:

3. The melodic leap of a major seventh has not been used a great deal by composers, although it does lend itself to "yearning" types of melody:

4. Because of its "bite," the major seventh has become a favorite sound of contemporary composers. The first example below shows the piling up of dissonance by superimposing major sevenths. The second example shows a scherzo-like use of melodic major sevenths:

5. The major seventh can be combined with other intervals to provide an harmonic background:

d. In the major scale, the major seventh can be built diatonically only on the first and fourth scale degrees. Continue the following exercise through the circle of fifths:

e. In the harmonic minor scale, diatonic major sevenths occur on the first, third, and sixth scale degrees. Continue the following exercise through the circle of fifths:

f. In the natural minor scale, diatonic major sevenths occur only on scale degrees 3 and 6. Continue this exercise through the circle of fifths:

g. Complete the following sequences by playing each pattern until the starting tone has been reached again. Analyze, melodically and harmonically, the intervals being used before trying to play the patterns:

EXERCISE 15: The Tritone: Augmented Fourth or Diminished Fifth

The **tritone** (discussed previously in Chapter 4) is the interval that divides the octave exactly in half. C up to F♯ (or G♭), for instance, encompasses the distance of three major seconds, or whole steps; from F♯ (or G♭) up to C also encompasses the distance of three major seconds. Depending upon how it is used, the tritone is written either as an augmented fourth (Aug. 4) or a diminished fifth (Dim. 5):

a. In the major scale, the tritone occurs between scale degrees 4 and 7, and 7 and 4:

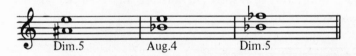

Transpose the following example to all other major keys:

b. In the natural minor, the tritone is found between scale degrees 2 and 6, and 6 and 2:

Transpose the following examples to six other minor keys:

c. The harmonic minor contains two sets of tritones, one between scale degrees 2 and 6 and 6 and 2, the other between scale degrees 4 and 7 and 7 and 4:

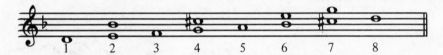

Transpose the following examples to six other minor keys:

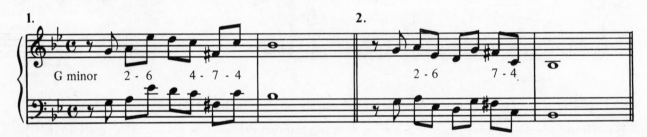

d. Play all the tritones in the major and minor scales of A, B^b, D, F$^\sharp$, E^b, C, B, and A^b.

e. Whether the tritone is written as an augmented fourth or a diminished fifth depends on how the interval resolves, or moves on. An augmented interval tends to resolve outward to a larger interval; a diminished interval tends to resolve inward to a smaller interval:

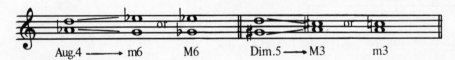

With the hands together, continue the following sequential patterns for one octave:

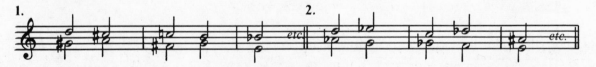

f. The tritone and its resolution moving above the circle of fifths in the bass is one of the most common—and basic—sounds of traditional harmony. Analyze the following sequential patterns, and continue each for two octaves:

EXERCISE 16: The Augmented Second and Diminished Seventh

The **augmented second** (Aug. 2) and its inversion, the **diminished seventh** (Dim. 7), occur diatonically only in the harmonic minor scale, between scale degrees 6 and 7, and 7 and 6:

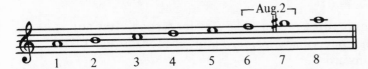

On the keyboard these intervals feel and sound like other, more usual intervals: the augmented second is the same size as the minor third; the diminished seventh is the same size as the major sixth:

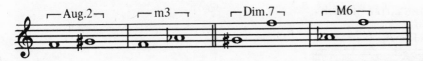

a. Practice playing augmented seconds and their inversions at random all over the keyboard.

b. Play the melodic progression 8-7-6-5-6-7-8 in the harmonic minor scales of G, B, C♯, E♭, and F.

c. Play the melodic progression 7-6-5-4-3-2-1, as shown below, in the harmonic minor keys of A, C, E, F, and B♭:

D minor   7   6   5   4   3   2   1

d. Analyze the following sequential patterns and continue each one for an octave:

e. Improvise musical ideas that feature the interval of the diminished seventh, as in this example:

EXERCISE 17: Less Usual Intervals: The Diminished Third; The Augmented Sixth; The Augmented Fifth

a. The **diminished third** (Dim. 3) feels and sounds on the keyboard like a major second. It is not a diatonic interval: it does not exist between the tones of any major, minor, or modal scale. Like most diminished intervals, it tends to resolve inward:

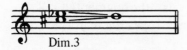

Play the following pattern through the circle of fifths:

b. The inversion of the diminished third is the **augmented sixth** (Aug. 6), which feels and sounds on the keyboard like a minor seventh:

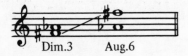

Like most augmented intervals, the augmented sixth tends to resolve outward:

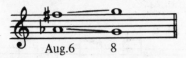

Continue the following sequential patterns for an octave:

c. Analyze the melodic and harmonic intervals in the following pattern. Then continue the pattern for two octaves:

d. Analyze this example, and continue it until the starting tones have been reached again:

e. The **augmented fifth** (Aug. 5) sounds and feels on the keyboard like a minor sixth:

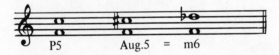

It occurs diatonically in the melodic and harmonic minor scales between scale degrees 3 and 7:

Continue this sequential pattern for one octave:

EXERCISE 18: Ear Training

a. Themes for ear memory:

1. Beethoven: Symphony No. 9, opening (*5th followed by 4th*)

2. William Schuman: *American Festival Overture*, principal theme (*m3*)

3. Tchaikovsky: Symphony No. 6 ("Pathétique"), third movement (*theme is made of 4ths*)

4. Wagner: *The Flying Dutchman*, opening theme (*4th and 5th*)

5. "Blue Room" (Rodgers and Hart) (*theme expands with a 4th, a 5th, a 6th, a 7th, an 8th*)

6. Verdi: *Aida*, "O Terra Addio" (*7th*)

Analyze the intervals in some of your favorite songs or symphonic themes.

b. Music to examine for interval content:

1. Hindemith: *Tanzstücke*, No. 1 (*4ths, octaves*)
   No. 2 (*3rds, 2nds, 7ths*)
   No. 4 (*2nds, 5ths, octaves*)

2. Milhaud: *Saudades do Brazil*, Vol. 2, No. 9, "Sumare" (*chords built in 4ths*)

3. Mompou: *Scènes d'Enfants*, "Cri dans la rue" (*chords in 4ths*)

4. Scriabin: Prélude, Opus 74, No. 3 (*M7ths in melody, tritone in bass*)

5. Shostakovich: *L'Age d'or*, "Polka" (*7ths, 9ths, etc.*)

6. Webern: Variationen für Klavier, Opus 27, No. 1 (*9ths, 7ths*)

c. Music featuring particular intervals; usage to be examined melodically and harmonically:

1. Chopin: Études, Opus 10, No. 7 (*3rds, 6ths*)
   No. 10 (*6ths*)
   Opus 25, No. 6 (*3rds, also Dim. 7ths*)
   No. 8 (*6ths*)
   Nos. 9 and 10 (*octaves*)

2. Debussy: Études, Vol. 1, No. 2 (*3rds*)
   No. 3 (*4ths*)
   No. 4 (*6ths*)
   No. 5 (*octaves*)

3. Bartók: Mikrokosmos, Vol. 2, pg. 20 (*5ths as accompaniment*)
   No. 56, "Melody in Tenths"
   No. 65, "Dialogue" (*5ths*)
   Vol. 4, No. 110, "Clashing Sounds" (*5ths and 3rds*)
   Vol. 5, No. 125, "Boating" (*4ths*)
   No. 131, "Fourths"
   No. 132, "Major Seconds Broken and Together"
   No. 134, "Studies in Double Notes" (*3rds, 2nds*)
   No. 135, "Perpetuum Mobile" (*3rds, 2nds*)
   Vol. 6, No. 142, "From the Diary of a Fly" (*2nds and others*)
   No. 144, "Minor Seconds and Major Sevenths"
   No. 147, "March" (*4ths, 5ths, octaves*)

Bagatelles, Opus 6, No. 2 (*2nds*)
>   No. 7 (*5ths and 2nds combined*)
>   No. 8 (*3rds*)
>   No. 11 (*chords built in 4ths*)
>   No. 14 (*2nds, 5ths, tritones, 3rds*)

Suite, Opus 14, No. 2 (*2nds*)
>   No. 3 (*4ths, 3rds, octaves*)

4. Riegger: *New and Old*, "Tone Clusters" (*2nds, 4ths, cluster*)
>   "Polytonality" (*4ths*)
>   "Fourths and Fifths"

7
CHORDS: TRIADS
Major; Minor; Diminished; Augmented; Polychords

A **chord** is a combination of three or more tones that are thought of and heard as a unit. A chord might be written as a vertical sound:

or the same tones might be sounded one at a time:

While chords can be made up of any combination of intervals, as shown in earlier chapters, certain traditional chord-building formulas have provided the basis of most European music.

The most common harmonic sound in music is the **triad**: a combination of three tones. There are four traditional types of triads, all built by superimposing major and minor thirds.

THE MAJOR TRIAD

The **major triad** is made by superimposing a minor third on a major third:

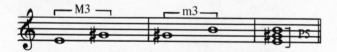

Note that the outer tones form a perfect fifth.

EXERCISE 1: The Major Triad

a. Play major triads by choosing a tone to be played by the left hand. With the right hand, play the tone which is a major third above the first tone; then add a tone which is a minor third above the second tone:

b. Play the major scale of C with the thumb of the right hand and the fifth finger of the left hand. Above each tone, play a major triad:

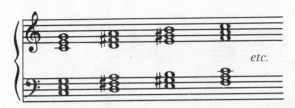

etc.

Repeat this exercise on the ascending and descending major scales of B^b, E, A^b, D, G^b, and B.

c. Find and play with both hands in various registers:

1. Those major triads whose tones are all on white keys.

2. Those whose tones are all on black keys.

3. Those whose middle tone is on a black key and whose outer tones are on white keys.

4. Those whose middle tone is on a white key and whose outer tones are on black keys.

5. The "odd" major triads on B^b and B.

EXERCISE 2: Naming and Using the Members of the Triad: Root, Third, Fifth

The tone on which a triad is built is known as the **root**; the middle tone is called the **third**, and the top tone the **fifth**:

Any tone can serve as a root, third, or fifth of a major triad:

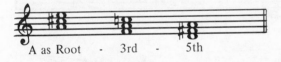

A as Root - 3rd - 5th

a. Choose tones at random on the keyboard. Play each tone as the root, the third, and the fifth of a major triad.

b. Improvise fanfare figures, as in the example below, using one tone as root, third, and fifth, although not necessarily in that order. Then move to another tone and treat it similarly:

c. Starting on the C-major triad, play a series of major triads whose roots follow the circle of fifths until C is reached again. The example below shows some of the ways this can be done. Continue the given patterns, and invent others:

d. Continue the following sequential patterns, first analyzing the interval relationships between the roots of the triads:

4.

Improvise short pieces using triads that progress as in the above examples.

e. It is important to be able to play a triad starting from any one of its members:

1. Choose a tone and think of it as the third of a major triad. Follow it by the fifth and the root of the triad, as in the example below. Practice, alternating hands, until each hand can play any major triad almost automatically:

2. Repeat this exercise in all registers of the keyboard, thinking of each starting tone as the fifth of the triad, to be followed by the root and the third:

EXERCISE 3: Triads in Open and Closed Position

When the tones of a triad lie within the interval of an octave, the triad is said to be in **close** or **closed position**:

When the tones of the triad are spread over a distance greater than an octave, the triad is said to be in **open position**:

a. Practice building major triads in open position (as illustrated in the first two measures of each example below), on the following bass notes:

b. Improvise short lyrical pieces and études based on the sound of the major triad in closed and open position.

EXERCISE 4: Major-Triad Polychords

Two major triads may be combined to form a **polychord**:

Against a C-major triad in the left hand, play other major triads with the right hand in order to explore different polychordal sounds. Use open and closed positions of both triads; play with hands close together, at various distances from each other, and in all registers. All polychordal sounds will not be equally pleasing. Select your favorites, and improvise melodic lines that grow out of them. The following examples can be used as style samples, and any two triads can be substituted for those given. Do not move away from your first polychord until you have exploited it thoroughly:

EXERCISE 5: Diatonic Major Triads

Capital Roman numerals, **I, IV, V**, etc., are used to represent major triads.

a. Diatonic major triads are found on the first, fourth, and fifth degrees of the major scale:

With the hands together, play the major triads in the keys of B^b, D, A^b, C$^\sharp$, and G^b.

b. In the harmonic minor scale, major triads are found on the fifth and sixth scale degrees:

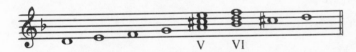

With the hands together, play the major triads to be found in the harmonic minor scales of F, D$^\sharp$, E, F$^\sharp$, G, and B. Play the triads in open and closed positions.

c. In the natural minor scale, major triads are found on the third, sixth, and seventh scale degrees:

With the hands together, play the major triads to be found in the natural minor scales of A, E^b, C$^\sharp$, B^b, and G$^\sharp$

THE MINOR TRIAD

The minor triad is made by superimposing a major third on a minor third, with the outer tones forming the interval of a perfect fifth:

EXERCISE 6: The Minor Triad

a. Practice playing minor triads by choosing a tone to be played by the left hand. With the right hand, play the tone which is a minor third above the first tone; then add the tone which is a major third above the second tone, as in the following example:

b. Play the natural minor scale of A with the thumb of the right hand and the little finger of the left hand. Make each tone of the scale the root of a minor triad:

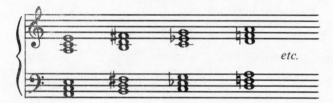

Repeat this exercise on the ascending and descending natural minor scales of D, F♯, B♭, C, F, and B.

c. Find and play, with both hands:

1. Those minor triads whose tones are all on the white keys.

2. Those whose tones are all on the black keys.

3. Those whose middle tone is a black key and whose outer tones are white keys.

4. Those whose middle tone is a white key and whose outer tones are black keys.

5. The "odd" minor triads on B♭ and B.

d. Starting on the C-minor triad, play a series of minor triads whose roots follow the circle of fifths until C is reached again:

e. Any tone can be the root, the third, or the fifth of a minor triad:

C as   Root   3rd   5th

1. Continue the following pattern, which shows tones used as root-third-fifth, through the circle of fifths, until the starting tone is reached again:

C as Root   3   5   F as Root   3   5   *etc.*

2. Continue the following idea, in which a melody tone is accompanied by minor triads. The melody tone serves as the root-third-fifth of the accompanying triads, although not necessarily in that order:

Slowly

E as R   3   5   G as R   3   5

f. Continue the following sequential patterns, first analyzing the intervallic relationship between the roots of the minor triads:

1.

etc.

2.

etc.

3.

etc.

g. Continue the following patterns, which use the minor triad in open as well as closed position:

EXERCISE 7: Diatonic Minor Triads

Lower-case Roman numerals, ii, iii, vi, etc., are used to represent minor triads.

a. Diatonic minor triads are found on the second, third, and sixth degrees of the major scale:

With the hands together, play the minor triads of the major keys of B, A^b, G, E, and F.

b. In the harmonic minor scale, minor triads are found on the first and fourth degrees of the scale:

With the hands together, play in closed and open position the minor triads to be found in the harmonic minor scales of F$^\sharp$, B^b, E^b, G$^\sharp$, C, and F.

c. In the natural minor scale, minor triads are found on the first, fourth, and fifth scale degrees:

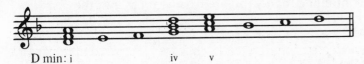

D min: i   iv   v

With the hands together, play in open and closed positions the minor triads to be found in the natural minor scales of G, B, D, A♭, C♯, and F♯.

EXERCISE 8: Improvising with Minor Triads

a. Analyze and expand the following examples:

b. The minor triads built on D, E, and A use only white keys. They can be used in various combinations to suggest modal scales. Expand the first example below, which could be considered to be in the Aeolian or natural minor mode. Add melodies to the second example in the Dorian mode, and to the third example in the Phrygian mode.

c. Note the use of non-chordal tones in the melody below. They move by step and are called **passing tones** (P.T.). Expand the example, continuing to incorporate passing tones into the chord-outline melodic line:

d. One of the most rewarding kinds of improvisation is that which explores how much can be done with the sound of one minor triad. The example below shows the beginning of a prelude-like piece based on the A-minor triad. The triad opens out melodically by using neighboring tones as well as passing tones. Expand the example, which starts with a long pedal tone in the left hand, for at least twenty measures. Ultimately the left hand should also participate in the melodic movement:

EXERCISE 9: Minor-Triad Polychords

Minor triads can be used, as were major triads, to form polychords. Try combining left-hand and right-hand minor triads at various intervals. Play the roots a second apart (F minor and G minor), a third apart (F minor and A minor), etc. Following are a few suggestions which should be expanded:

a. Move from one minor triad to another in primarily step-wise fashion, as in a hymn:

b. Use polychords in a syncopated rhythmic pattern:

c. Improvise other musical ideas based on minor polychords.

EXERCISE 10: Combining Major and Minor Triads to Make Polychords

Major and minor triads can be combined, as in the example below in which a right-hand melody
based on a C-major triad is accompanied, to create a polychordal texture, by a series of minor
triads in the left hand:

Improvise dance forms, études, and lyrical pieces based on four types of polychords:

Major-major
Minor-major
Minor-minor
Major-minor

EXERCISE 11: Ear Training

The following list contains major or minor triads used as significant thematic openings. Try to play
these openings, and continue the pieces as far as you can. Think of, and play, other examples of
major and minor triads used melodically in other music you know.

1.   "The Star-Spangled Banner"

2.   "Steal Away"

3.   "Black is the Color of My True Love's Hair"

4.   Mendelssohn: *Elijah*, "It Is Enough"

5.   "La Cucaracha"

6.   Chopin: Prélude No. 24

7.   "I Could Have Danced All Night," from *My Fair Lady* (Lerner and Loewe)

8.   "Happy Days Are Here Again" (Ager and Yellen)

9.   Brahms: Hungarian Dance No. 5

10.   Wagner: *Walküre*, "The Ride of the Valkyries"

11.   Strauss: *The Blue Danube* Waltz No. 1

12.   Beethoven: Piano Sonata, Opus 2, No. 1

13.   Beethoven: Piano Sonata, Opus 27, No. 2

14.   Beethoven: Piano Sonata, Opus 57 ("Appassionata")

15.   Wagner: *Der Ring des Nibelungen*, "Siegfried's Horn Call"

16.   Mendelssohn: Symphony No. 4 ("Italian")

17.   Haydn: Symphony No. 94 ("Surprise"), slow movement

18.   Brahms: Symphony No. 4

19.   Mozart: Piano Sonata, K. 457

20.   Mozart: Piano Sonata, K. 545

THE DIMINISHED TRIAD

The **diminished triad** is made by combining two minor thirds:

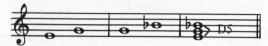

Note that the interval made by the root and the fifth is a diminished fifth.

EXERCISE 12: The Diminished Triad

a. Play diminished triads by choosing a tone to be played by the left hand. With the right hand, play the tone which is a minor third above the first tone; then add another minor third above the second tone:

b. Play the descending and ascending scale of C major with the index finger of the left hand. Add to each tone the two tones that will complete a diminished triad, played melodically by the right hand:

Repeat this exercise in the scales of B^b and E major; G and D harmonic minor; and F$^\sharp$ and C natural minor.

c. Continue the following sequential patterns:

d. The diminished triad is used much less than the major and minor triads. Its distinctive sound is, however, capable of being used for quite interesting effects. Improvise musical ideas based principally on the diminished triad, as in the examples below. Expand each example:

1. A "thumb-line" melody moves chromatically over a chromatic, long-tone bass:

2. The diminished triad has been used for an "agitato" effect:

3. A melodic line suggesting the Locrian mode, in which each tone of the diminished triad is preceded by its lower or upper neighboring tone:

EXERCISE 13: Diatonic Diminished Triads

Diminished triads are indicated with lower-case Roman numerals and a °: vii°, ii°, etc.

a. There is only one diminished triad in the major scale. It is found on the seventh degree of the scale:

Continue this pattern through the circle of fifths:

b. Diminished triads are found on the second and seventh degrees of the harmonic minor scale. Continue this pattern through the circle of fifths:

c. In the natural minor scale, the diminished triad is found on the second scale degree. Play the following pattern in the keys of E, B♭, F♯, G, and C♯ natural minor:

THE AUGMENTED TRIAD

The **augmented triad** (which was introduced in Chapter 4) is made by superimposing a major third on a major third. The interval between the root and the fifth is an augmented fifth:

EXERCISE 14: The Augmented Triad

a. Review augmented triads by choosing a tone at random, played by the left hand. With the right hand play the tone that lies a major third above the first tone; then add another tone which lies a major third above the second tone:

b. Play the F-major scale with the thumb of the right hand and the fifth finger of the left hand. Make each scale tone the root of an augmented triad:

Repeat this exercise in the ascending and descending major scales of A, E♭, B, D, and A♭, and the harmonic minor scales of G, B, C, F♯, and D.

c. Analyze the following sequential patterns. Practice the patterns one hand at a time, then with the hands together. Continue each one until the original tones are reached again. Invent original sequential patterns based on the augmented triad.

d. The augmented triad is the basic triad of the whole-tone scale. Debussy used it as such in many works, including the Prélude from his suite *Pour le Piano*:

e. Analyze and continue the following fragments:

3.

4.

EXERCISE 15: The Diatonic Augmented Triad

Augmented triads are indicated by large Roman numerals followed by a + sign.

Diatonically, the augmented triad occurs only in the harmonic minor. It is found on the third scale degree. Starting in C harmonic minor, play through the circle of fifths using the first five tones of each scale, and placing an augmented triad on the third degree of each scale:

EXERCISE 16: Types of Triads in Combination

A single tone has twelve triadic relationships: it can be considered as root-third-fifth of a major, a minor, a diminished, and an augmented triad. Complete the following patterns, going through the circle of fifths: after playing the tone C in all its triadic relationships, move on to F, B^b, E^b, etc.

a. Play these examples in a steady rhythmic pattern:

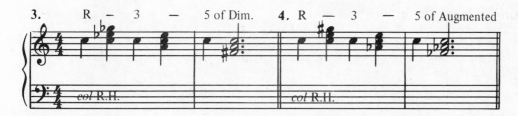

b. Invent variants of the above, such as playing the triads as broken chords in quintuplets, as in the first example below, or embellishing chord tones with neighboring tones, as in the second example:

c. Starting on the C-major triad, play triads of varying kinds through the circle of fifths. Play the triads consistently in the same order, for example, major-minor-diminished-augmented. Repeat, starting on D, E^b, and F major:

d. Moving through the circle of fifths, decorate each chord tone with its lower neighboring tone, as shown below. Invent your own order of triadic types:

EXERCISE 17: Examples from Music

As with all musical materials, triads can become anything that a composer wishes to make of them. Haydn, for example, uses a major triad as the basic thematic material for many of his symphonic movements:

Symphony No. 32
Allegro molto

Symphony No. 38
Allegro molto

Symphony No. 50
Adagio

Symphony No. 56
Allegro molto

Symphony No. 82 ("The Bear")
Allegro

Beethoven's Symphony No. 3 ("Eroica") opens with an expanded statement of an E-flat major triad:

Debussy and Puccini use triads almost like single melody tones:

Debussy: *Pour le Piano*, **Prélude**

Assez animé et très rythmé

non legato

Puccini: *La Bohème*

Allegro focoso

EXERCISE 18: Improvising with Triads

The following triadic musical ideas should be used as the basis of expanded improvisations:

a. Both hands play a triadic design using only white keys:

b. A slow, open melody drifts over an ostinato:

c. A chromatic melody has a slightly ominous quality when put in the lower register and accompanied by different types of triads. In this example, the right hand plays the third and fifth tones of the triads, the left hand the root and the fifth:

d. The improvisor can establish limitations or ground rules for his improvisations. In this example, ascending melodic motion uses major triads, while descending motion is accompanied by minor triads. After a bit, the "rule" could be reversed so that minor triads accompany upward motion, and major triads the downward line:

e. Two streams of triads, one in close position, the other in open position, can be treated like two melodies moving, for the most part, in contrary motion. Note that major and minor triads are mixed together:

f. Chromatically descending triadic melody lines alternate with another group of triads over an ostinato:

g. A triad and the lower neighbor of its root can be woven into an interesting keyboard pattern:

h. Polychordal harmonic sounds result from setting up an ostinato in the right hand, in this case using a triad in open position, while the left hand moves slowly in major and minor triads in open position:

Remember that much improvisation is based on trial and error. This is especially true in dealing with triads. Not everything will sound well. Sometimes, if the rhythm is maintained, things will straighten out; if not, start again with a modification of the original idea. Be in control at all times. Know what you are doing, and be able to recall the improvisation, at least in general outline, after you have finished.

EXERCISE 19: Inversions of Triads

a. Play the tones of the C-major triad, with C as the lowest tone; move the hand so that E is the bottom tone, then G:

The arrangement of the tones of a chord with a tone other than the root as the lowest tone is called **inversion**. When the third of a triad is the lowest tone, the triad is said to be in its **first inversion**:

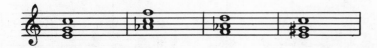

b. Play the following series of root-position triads; follow each triad with its first inversion:

c. Continue the following example, which shows the diatonic triads in the key of C major first in root position, then in first inversion. Repeat this exercise in the keys of G harmonic minor, A^b major, D harmonic minor, E major, and F natural minor:

d. Play the scale of G major in the upper voice in both the left and right hands. Below each tone arrange a major triad in first inversion:

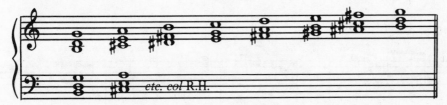

1. Repeat the exercise above, making each chord a minor triad.

2. Play a major triad in first inversion beneath each scale tone in the keys of A harmonic minor, D melodic minor, and G natural minor.

e. Continue the following sequences until the starting tone is reached again. Practice hands separately,
   then together. When the fifth is in the bass, the triad is in **second inversion**.

1.

2.

f. Analyze, then continue this étude until the starting chord has been reached again:

Repeat the étude in the keys of D major, E^b major, G harmonic minor, and E natural minor.

g. Continue the following patterns until the starting triad is reached again. Practice hands separately,
   then together:

h. Continue the following musical ideas based on the use of triads in various inversions and spacings.
For variety, change key, and change the direction of basses or melodies:

i. Experiment with polychords, combining major and minor triads in inversions. Analyze and
    expand the following:

8

SEVENTH
AND NINTH CHORDS

While the triad has been the basic harmonic sound in Western European music since 1400, composers have enriched the sound of the triad by adding one or more tones to it, thus converting the triad into a seventh chord or a ninth chord.

SEVENTH CHORDS

The **seventh chord** is a four-tone chord consisting of a triad plus a tone that lies either a major third or a minor third above the top tone of a triad. It is called a seventh chord because its top tone lies at the distance of a seventh above the root of the chord:

EXERCISE 1: Constructing the Several Seventh Chords

a. Play triads consecutively on each tone of the major scales of G, B^b, F, and A. Add the tone which is a diatonic third above the top tone of each triad, making a series of diatonic seventh chords:

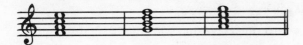

D: I7   ii7   iii7   IV7   V7   vi7   vii°7   I7

b. The chords on the first and fourth scale degrees are *major triads* plus a *major third*. This form of seventh chord is called a **major seventh** chord (maj. 7):

I7   IV7

Play major seventh chords built on E^b, F$^\sharp$, A^b, G, and B.

c. The chord on the fifth scale degree is a *major triad* plus a *minor third*. This is called a **dominant seventh** chord (dom. 7):

Play dominant sevenths built on E, C, B^b, A, and D^b.

d. On the second, third, and sixth scale degrees are *minor triads* plus a *minor third*. This form of the seventh chord is called a **minor seventh** chord (min. 7):

Play minor sevenths built on D, F, A, B^b, and G$^\sharp$.

e. On the seventh scale degree is a *diminished triad* plus a *major third*. This is called a **half-diminished seventh** chord (ϕ7):

Play half-diminished sevenths built on F$^\sharp$, B, G, A, and D.

f. The **diminished seventh** chord (dim. 7) has been presented earlier as a series of minor thirds. It can also be thought of as a *diminished triad* plus a *minor third*.

EXERCISE 2: Improvising with Seventh Chords

a. Play the scale of C major. Build a major seventh chord on each tone, continuing the following example with chords in both hands:

Build major seventh chords on each tone of these scales: A harmonic minor, C melodic minor, B^b natural minor.

b. Build dominant seventh chords on each tone of these scales: E major, F harmonic minor, G melodic minor, B natural minor.

c. Build minor seventh chords above each tone of these scales: A major, E harmonic minor, B^b melodic minor, C$^\sharp$ natural minor.

d. Build half-diminished seventh chords on each tone of these scales: E^b major, G$^\sharp$ harmonic minor, F melodic minor, D natural minor.

e. Build diminished seventh chords on each tone of these scales: A^b major, D$^\sharp$ harmonic minor, A melodic minor, E natural minor.

f. The following example shows all five types of usual seventh chords, as built on one tone: C.
Repeat the series on D, A^b, E, B^b, and F$^\sharp$:

g. Analyze the following sequences, and continue them until the starting tone is reached again:

h. Continue the following sequences through the circle of fifths. Play each of the first three patterns,
first with dominant seventh chords, then with minor sevenths, then with alternating dominant
sevenths and minor sevenths as in No. 4:

i. Diatonic seventh chords may be used in various ways. Here are some to experiment with:

1. One of the most common spacings of seventh chords is with the root and the fifth in the left hand, the third and the seventh in the right hand. Continue this idea, using diatonic seventh chords, for some time, always keeping the same shape in the hands:

2. Practice diatonic seventh chords in open position in the left hand until the shape of the seventh becomes automatic under the hand. Then add a melodic line in the right hand:

EXERCISE 3: Inversions of the Seventh Chord

The seventh chord can be used in four positions: root, first inversion, second inversion, and third inversion. Note that in the inversions of a seventh chord there is always the interval of a second. When trying to determine which chord member is the root of the seventh chord, find the interval of a second. The upper note of the second will be the root of the chord.

a. On each of the given bass notes, build the type of seventh chord indicated, and play it in all positions as illustrated:

1. Major seventh

2. Minor seventh

3. Dominant seventh

4. Half-diminished seventh

b. The following pattern consists of a series of seventh chords. Each chord moves from its root position to its three possible inversions. The sequence of types of seventh chords is indicated. After learning the pattern, repeat it using seventh chords built on B^b, E, A^b, D, and G:

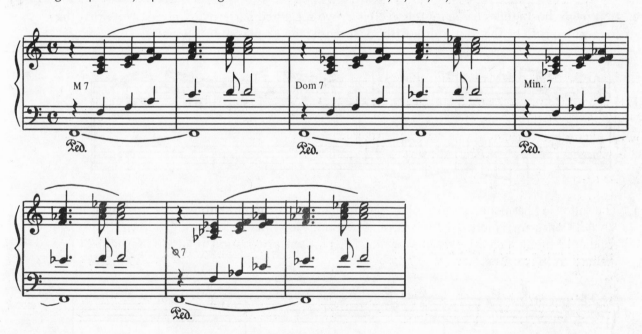

c. Parallel seventh chords in inversion may be used to harmonize simple melodies. The example below shows the melody of the French song, "Sur le Pont d'Avignon" harmonized with the melody tone always used as the root of a diatonic seventh chord. The other tones of the chord are played below the melody tone in close position, so that the seventh chords are always in first inversion:

The same technique may be used with the seventh chords in second and third inversions. Always keep the hand in the same position of the chord:

Play simple melodies, harmonizing them with parallel seventh chords. Treat each melody tone as the root, third, or fifth of a seventh chord, as shown above.

d. Use a tone as the root, third, fifth, and seventh of a series of dominant sevenths, as shown here in the bass:

Repeat the exercise above on D, B^b (A$^\sharp$), C, and E.

e. Improvise short études based on this exercise; two suggested patterns are given. Note that the tone which is to be the root, third, fifth, or seventh may be played in any voice.

f. The following harmonic progression is based on a progression of diatonic seventh chords in a Vivaldi Concerto. Practice the progression begun in No. 1 below, continuing down the D-major scale until the first chord is reached again. Then use the progression as an accompaniment to a melody, as in No. 2 below:

EXERCISE 4: Less Usual Seventh Chords

In addition to the five types of seventh chords that are most commonly used, there are other possibilities.

a. Certain unusual seventh chords occur diatonically in minor. Continue this sequence of diatonic sevenths to be found in the ascending melodic minor scale. Analyze the types of seventh chords which occur on the first and third scale degrees:

1.   Transpose the pattern above to the ascending melodic minor scales of G, B, E, and F.

2.   Improvise musical ideas based on the type of seventh chord found on the first scale degree of the melodic minor.

3.   Improvise musical ideas based on the type of seventh chord found on the third scale degree of the melodic minor.

b. A dominant seventh is occasionally used with a raised fifth degree. Here is an harmonic phrase by Gershwin in which this type of seventh is used twice. Play the phrase; analyze the movement of the voices, and repeat the phrase starting on the four triads indicated:

c. The dominant seventh is commonly found used with a lowered fifth, particularly in certain jazz styles:

This chord is one of the whole-tone combinations studied earlier; it will also appear later, in traditional harmony, as one form of the augmented sixth chord. It is often used in second inversion, with the lowered fifth in the lowest voice. (In guitar and jazz terminology the word is "flatted," or "flat" fifth.) Analyze the following sequential pattern and continue it through the circle of fifths:

d. Seventh chords provide much rich sound to experiment with. After continuing the opening measures that follow, improvise freely with all types of sevenths. The first fragment below shows a highly chromatic melody over a series of dominant sevenths moving through the circle of fifths. The second shows a series of different types of sevenths arrived at by moving the voices chromatically. This series could also move through the circle of fifths.

NINTH CHORDS

A **ninth chord** is a five-tone chord made by adding another tone to a seventh chord. The additional tone lies a major or minor third above the top tone of the seventh chord, and thus a major or minor ninth above the root of the chord:

EXERCISE 5: Improvising with Ninth Chords

a. Play the diatonic ninth chords in the scale of F major, continuing the spacing shown below. This spacing, with the root and fifth of the chord in the left hand, is the one which has been used most often:

Repeat the exercise above in the major keys of D, B^b, E, and C$^{\sharp}$.

b. Improvise on the sounds of dominant sevenths with major or minor ninths, as in these examples:

1. Slowly

2.

c. Play simple melodies, making each melody tone the top of a ninth chord. Choose one type of ninth chord to be used throughout:

1. "Mary Had a Little Lamb"   2. "Yankee Doodle"

9

MUSICAL SHORTHAND
Figured Bass; Guitar-Chord Symbols

FIGURED BASS

Figured bass is a traditional form of musical shorthand. Invented in the late 1500's, and used consistently throughout the Baroque era, it is a notational system that saves the composer the trouble of writing out all the notes of a chordal accompaniment to a melody. A set of numbers and symbols, usually written below the notes of a bass line (although in the Baroque era, composers often wrote the numbers and symbols above the bass line, or even beside it), tells the keyboard player what tones, and thus what chords, are to be played above the bass.

The process of playing from a figured bass is known as "realizing a figured bass." Skilled keyboard players learn to realize quickly the chords indicated, and even to improvise imitative and contrasting contrapuntal lines to blend with the melodic lines above them.

In realizing a figured bass, the player is responsible for almost everything except the basic harmonic progression (provided by the composer through the bass line and the figures) and the basic rhythm. He can decide for himself how to distribute the required tones on the keyboard, in what octave to play a given tone, what tone or tones to omit, what tone or tones to double, etc. In its highest form, realizing a figured bass accompaniment can become an artistic achievement, almost equal to composition.

The principles of realizing a figured bass are fairly simple; with practice and experience, the player can learn to produce results that are sophisticated. For practical purposes, the player should accept a few basic assumptions:

1. The harmonies indicated or implied by a figured bass are triadic, that is, chords built in thirds: triads, sevenths, even ninth chords.

2. The arabic figures written below (or above) the bass notes tell the keyboard player how far above the bass the desired notes lie: a 5 means that the note is 5 tones up, or a fifth; 3 means a third; 6 means a sixth, 4 means a fourth, etc.

3. Customarily the figures are written in a vertical column, in descending order, with the highest number (representing the widest interval) at the top of the column.

4. A figured bass assumes the use of the tones within the diatonic scale of the key signature, unless a chromatic alteration is indicated.

EXERCISE 1: The Triad in Root Position in Figured Bass

A triad in root position is indicated by the figure $\frac{5}{3}$:

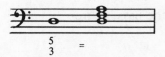

Since the root-position triad itself is so common and so well understood, composers often omitted the figures for it, trusting the competency of the performer to fill in this obvious harmony. A bass note standing alone, without figures, can be assumed to be the root of a triad:

The use of a note a third above the bass, like the use of a root-position triad, is so common that, again, composers customarily omitted the figure, assuming the player would understand it was implied. Thus, a chromatic sign (♯, ♭, or ♮) refers to the tone that lies a third above the bass tone. In root position, this will be third of the triad:

The tones above the bass note often can be played most conveniently by the right hand. They may be distributed in various ways:

Realize the following bass lines in as simple a fashion as possible. In general, try to move the right hand in contrary motion to the bass line. After realizing each bass line in a simplified version, experiment with broken chords and arpeggios. Play each example several times, starting each time with a different chord tone in the soprano part:

EXERCISE 2: The Triad in First Inversion

The first inversion of a triad is indicated by the figure $\frac{6}{3}$, often abbreviated to 6, since the 3 is implied and understood. If the tone that lies a sixth above the bass is to be chromatically altered, the chromatic sign will be written either before or after the number: $^{\sharp}\frac{6}{3}$ or $\frac{6\sharp}{3}$ or $^{\flat}\frac{6}{3}$, etc. (In old scores, the raised sixth is sometimes indicated by a slash: ⑥.) Usually the bass tone of a first inversion (which is the third of the chord) is not doubled in the right hand, unless the sixth above the bass is chromatically altered, as in No. 2 below:

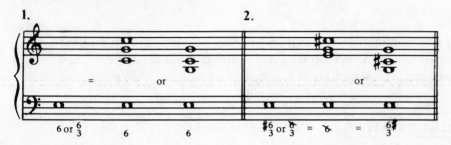

Realize the following bass lines which call for triads in root position or first inversion:

EXERCISE 3: The Triad in Second Inversion

A second-inversion triad is indicated by the figure $\frac{6}{4}$. The tones above the bass can be treated like those of a triad in root position. Realize the following basses which call for triads in root position, first inversion, and second inversion:

EXERCISE 4: Adding Non-Chordal Tones to a Figured-Bass Realization

A figured bass can generate or suggest several melodies that use both chord tones and non-chord tones. Here is a sample bass line:

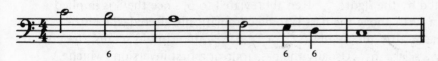

Here it is realized with a melody that consists of chord tones. Each of these melody tones, if played in close position with the bass, is either a third or a sixth away from the bass:

Here the melody is embellished with non-chordal neighboring and passing tones:

Here an inner voice, consisting of chord tones, is added:

Improvise melodic solutions to the figured basses given in Exercises 2 and 3 above.

EXERCISE 5: Realizing a Figured Bass When the Melody Is Given

Following are some melodies and their figured basses. Fill in, below the melody tones, the chord tones indicated by the figured bass. In some cases, one added tone is enough; in others, two tones may be added. Experiment to see how *few* tones are needed between the soprano and bass lines:

3. Purcell (abridged)

EXERCISE 6: The Seventh Chord in Figured Bass

The notation of seventh chords in figured bass follows the principles of the notation of triads. The various positions are noted as follows (the numbers in parentheses are often omitted):

The example below shows the four positions of a seventh chord built on G:

Realize the following figured basses which emphasize seventh chords.

1.

4. Bach: Chorale, "Herzliebster Jesu, was hast du"

5. Bach: Chorale, "Nun lob', mein Seel', den Herren"

GUITAR-CHORD SYMBOLS

Another system of notational shorthand is the use of **guitar-chord symbols**. In many editions of popular songs and folk songs, the harmony is indicated by the use of letter names, plus other symbols. All the player needs to do is to distribute the tones of the given chord in whatever order sounds best to him, or is the easiest order to play on his instrument. The guitar-chord symbols can easily be translated to the keyboard, usually by playing the chord in root position. Here is the way that the various types of triads and seventh chords built on G would be indicated:

Triads

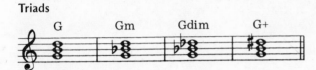

Seventh chords

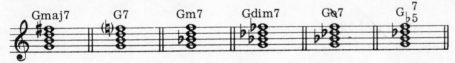

EXERCISE 7: Realizing Guitar-Chord Symbols

Play the indicated chords as repeated chords, with the root of the chord in the left hand, as shown. Move from one chord to the next as smoothly as possible:

1. 4/4:   C/G7/Am/Em/Cmaj7/Gm7/Am/Em/Fmaj7-G7/C/Ab7/Dm7/G7/C

2. 4/4:   Dm7/G7/Am/Cmaj7/Dm7/G7/Am/C/Bb/Bbmaj7/Bb7/Ebmaj7/C#dim7/Dm7/G7/C

3. 4/4:   A-F#m/D-E7/A-F#m/Dmaj7-E7/A/D/G/E7/A

4. 4/4:   Cm7-F7/Cm7-F7/Bbmaj7-Gm7/Bbmaj7-Gm7/Bb/Bb/Em7-A7/Dmaj7-Gmaj7/
          Cmaj7-Fm7/Bb7-Eb7/Abmaj7

5. 4/4:   G/Gmaj7/F/F7/Bb/Bbmaj7/Ab/Db/Db7/Gbmaj7/Ebm7-Ab7/Db/E7/A/D7/G7/C

After realizing the guitar chords, improvise melodies that are generated by the chords.

PART III
Traditional Harmony

10

THE TONIC, THE DOMINANT, AND THE SUB-DOMINANT
Authentic Cadences; Improvisation in Traditional Harmony; The Alberti Bass; Plagal Cadences

Traditional harmony is the name given to those procedures such as chord progression, voice-leading, doubling, etc., that have been observed in the musical practices of the composers who wrote between 1650 and 1850. Many of these procedures were in use before 1650, and many are still in use today; but within the given two-hundred-year span, they dominated musical practices.

THE TONIC AND DOMINANT HARMONIES

Essentially, traditional harmony consists of stating the **tonic** chord (I or i), the home or "rest" chord, built on the first degree of the scale; moving away from that chord; and ultimately arriving back at the tonic. The moving away can take a long time and involve many chords, or it can be a simple matter of moving from the tonic to the **dominant** (V or V7), the chord built on the fifth degree of the scale, and thence back to the tonic.

EXERCISE 1: Finding the Tonic and Dominant Seventh Within a Scale

The tonic chord consists of scale degrees 1-3-5:

The dominant triad consists of scale degrees 5-7-2; the dominant seventh (V^7) is made up of scale degrees 5-7-2-4:

a. Find and play the I, V, and V⁷ in the keys of B harmonic minor, E major, A♭ major, D harmonic minor, F# major, B♭ harmonic minor. Follow the pattern of this example:

b. Over the root of a V⁷, practice playing the four positions of the chord in the right hand, as shown. Repeat in the major and minor keys indicated by the key signatures:

c. Make arpeggio patterns using the above V⁷ chords. Experiment with open and closed positions of the chord, with both hands in octaves, with the hands together but playing the chord in different positions:

EXERCISE 2: Dominant-Tonic (V-1) Resolutions

a. Play and analyze the following V-I progressions. Transpose the examples to at least six other major and minor keys:

b. Play and analyze the following pattern in which the four positions of the V^7 in the right hand resolve. Repeat, using E^b, B, F, D^b, A, and G^b as roots of V^7's:

Chords and their inversions will be designated as follows: Roman numerals will be used to indicate the scale degree on which the chord is built; figured-bass symbols will be used to indicate chord positions. I_6, for instance, represents the first inversion of a major tonic triad. V_2^4 represents the dominant seventh in third inversion.

c. Outline a series of V^7-I resolutions in F major, as shown below. In the left hand play only single tones: the root of a C^7 (or V^7 in F) on the first beat of the first bar; the third of a C^7 on the first beat of the second bar, etc. Resolve each V^7 bass tone to a I or a I_6 as shown, on the third beat of each bar. Play the other tones of each chord in the right hand. *Avoid doubling the third or the seventh of the V^7.* Improvise accompaniment patterns as shown in Nos. 2 and 3 below:

2.   3.

Repeat the above exercises in at least six other major or minor keys.

d. The spacings and resolutions given above do not by any means exhaust the possible ways in which the V^7 can resolve to I. Experiment and find at least three more possibilities.

e. Analyze the following example and continue it as a sequence through the circle of fifths until the starting point is reached again:

etc.

EXERCISE 3: Chord Members: The Shifting Functions of a Single Tone

A given tone can be considered as the root, third, fifth, or seventh of a V^7, and each V^7 can be resolved to its proper I, as in the example below:

A as root   A as 3rd

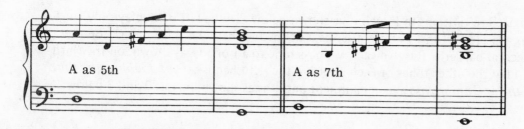

A as 5th   A as 7th

a. Repeat the above on A^b ($G^\sharp$), E^b ($D^\sharp$), F ($E^\sharp$), and G.

b. Consider a tone to be the seventh scale degree, or **leading tone**. Harmonize it with the V or V^7 of which it is the chord third; resolve the chord to its proper tonic:

Repeat the above on six other tones.

c. After playing these V⁷-I progressions in simple form, decorate them and make pianistic figurations, as shown below:

d. Continue this sequence in which each tonic tone becomes a new leading tone. Play the sequence in simple form, as in No. 1; then decorate it with the leading tone jumping over the tonic before resolving, as shown in No. 2:

Repeat the sequence above, making each tonic chord minor instead of major. Repeat again, alternating major and minor tonics.

e. Think of a tone as the second degree of a major or minor scale. Harmonize the tone with a V or a V⁷ and resolve:

f. Analyze and continue the following sequence based on the same principle. Make **enharmonic changes** when necessary:

g. Think of a tone as the fourth degree of a major or minor scale. Harmonize the tone as the seventh of a V^7, resolve it to the tonic:

Repeat the above on B^b, C, G, D^b, and A.

EXERCISE 4: Dominant-Tonic Sequences

a. Analyze the following sequential patterns and continue them until the starting tones are reached again:

b. Invent several other sequential patterns using V, V⁷ and I. (These are good ear-training exercises for the other members of the class, who should be asked to figure out the patterns.)

EXERCISE 5: Emphasis on Rhythmic Patterns

Below are several sets of rhythmic and harmonic patterns.   Play the indicated chords in the right hand; in the left hand, play the root of each chord, as shown in this example:

EXERCISE 6: Realizing Tonic-Dominant Figured Basses

Realize the following figured basses which use I, V, and V^7 chords. Above the bass let the other tones move as smoothly as possible from one chord to the next. Try for contrary motion and an interesting, though simple, melody:

THE AUTHENTIC CADENCE

The **authentic cadence** is basically the progression of a V or a V^7 to a I at the end of a musical work, or the end of a section of a work.

EXERCISE 7: The Perfect Authentic Cadence

The **perfect authentic cadence**, which is used for a sense of finality, is one in which the roots of the V and the I are in the bass, and the root of the tonic is doubled in the soprano:

a. Play each of the following perfect authentic cadences, which occur at the end of compositions. Analyze each example, noting spacing, doubling, and melodic decoration. Transpose each example to at least three other keys:

b. Play a descending major scale, continuing down beyond the octave to scale degrees 7 and 8. Use these tones as the soprano part of a perfect authentic cadence. Either the V or the V^7 may be used to precede the I:

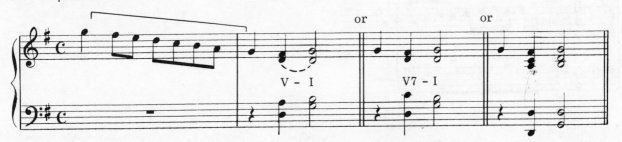

Repeat this example in at least three major and three harmonic minor keys.

EXERCISE 8: The Imperfect Authentic Cadence

An **imperfect authentic cadence** is one in which the harmonic progression follows the dominant-tonic pattern, but the roots of the chords are not necessarily in the bass. In an imperfect authentic cadence, the melody need not end on the keynote, or tonic. Play and analyze the following examples of imperfect cadences. Transpose them to at least four other major or minor keys:

IMPROVISATION IN TRADITIONAL HARMONY

Improvisation within traditional harmony is based on the compositional principle that harmony can generate, influence, and dictate melody.

An harmonic sound may be thought of as occupying a certain amount of time-space. Any number of melodic lines can be fitted into that space, *as long as each melodic line is based on the chord occupying that time-space*. The space itself might be one beat, one measure, or several measures. The following brief excerpts illustrate the principle.

The example below shows how Bach combines two melodic strands based on an F-major triad. The right hand outlines the descending triad; chord tones are connected by passing tones and upper neighbors. In the left hand, the pure triad is unfolded rhythmically:

Bach: *Two-Part Invention* No. 8

The next example shows how a G-minor triad can become four lines for chorus plus an orchestral accompaniment. The vocal lines are built exclusively on the tones of the triad. The orchestral parts are also built on the G-minor triad, but with upper and lower neighboring tones decorating each chord tone. The bass insistently repeats the root of the triad:

Bach: *St. John Passion*

EXERCISE 9: Improvising on the Tonic-Dominant Harmonic Outline of a Schubert Waltz

Utilizing the principle discussed above, the harmonic plan of a Schubert waltz, for example, can be used to make an almost limitless number of new melodies.

a. Play this Schubert Waltz several times, and analyze the harmonic scheme:

b. Practice playing the harmonic plan of the Schubert Waltz in several ways, such as:

c. Following the eight-measure harmonic plan of the Schubert Waltz, improvise melodies generated by the harmonies. The given fragments should be completed, and several more melodic lines in each category should be invented:

1. Make melodies using only chord tones:

2. Mix a few neighboring tones among the chord tones:

3. Connect chord tones by means of passing tones. These can be diatonic or chromatic:

4. Use non-harmonic tones which are approached by leap and resolved by step. Such tones are called **appoggiaturas** by modern theorists:

5. Introduce **suspension tones** when moving from one chord to another. A suspension is a tone that is held over from a previous harmony; in the new harmony it becomes a non-chordal tone before resolving. A suspension has three parts: the preparation, in which the tone appears as a chord member; the suspension itself, when the harmony shifts while the tone is held; and the resolution, when the suspension moves on by step (usually downward, but occasionally upward) to resolve. A suspension may occur in any voice; for the present, use it only in the melodic line:

6. The melody tones may be paralleled in the right hand at intervals of the third or the sixth:

EXERCISE 10: Changing the Rhythmic Patterns

Other dance forms can be built on the harmonic plan of the Schubert waltz by changing the rhythmic patterns. Complete the following fragments in which:

a. A *mazurka* can be made by using rhythmic patterns such as ♩. ♫ ♩ ♩ or ♩ ♩ that throw an accent on the second beat. Note that the mode is now minor:

b. A *polka* results from putting the rhythmic pattern ♪ | ♫ ♪ in the melody, and ♫ ♩ in the accompaniment. Note that the meter has been changed from triple to duple:

c. The harmonic plan can become a *tango* or *habanera* by putting a slightly syncopated melody over this rhythmic accompaniment:

d. A *tarantella* is an exciting dance, with running triplets in the melody and an insistent rhythmic accompaniment. In the example below, each chord lasts for two measures, doubling the length of the original pattern. A **pedal point** on G adds a bit of dissonance to the V^7. (A pedal point is a tone or tones that hold or sound continually while the surrounding harmony keeps changing.)

EXERCISE 11: Improvising Alberti Bass Accompaniments

Inversions of the V^7 can be used so that less distance needs to be covered in the left hand. Here the harmonic plan of the Schubert Waltz has been slightly altered to become $I-V_6-V_4^3-I$:

The following examples show the activation of the tones in the accompaniment style known as the **Alberti bass**, used by Mozart and other composers of the Classical period:

Improvise several melodic variants, accompanied by Alberti basses, on the I-V-V-I harmonic pattern of the Schubert Waltz.

EXERCISE 12: Taking the Melody Out of the Soprano

The melody does not always have to be in the soprano:

a. A Schumannesque "thumb duet," with the melody in the middle, can be made by paralleling a simple chord-tone melody in thirds, with other tones of the chords weaving above and below the melody:

b. The melody may be in the left hand, with the accompaniment in the right. Complete this beginning, and improvise other left-hand melodies:

EXERCISE 13: Extending the Tonal Range Beyond the Hand Span

In the Alberti bass and other accompaniment styles used before 1800, the chord tones were arranged so that they fitted under the hand. When the tonal resources of the pedal were added to the piano, a whole new set of resonances and textures became possible. In brief, the keyboard was thought of as having three main registers: the bass, the alto-tenor middle, and the treble. By using the pedal, the pianist is able, in effect, to "stretch" his hand. The pedal can sustain a bass tone, which has the greatest amount of resonance and richness, while the player fills in other tones of a chord in the middle register, meanwhile floating a melody on top of the bass and the chord. Diagrammed, the registers of the piano look like this:

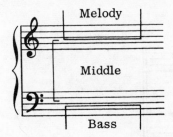

Improvise a nocture, or barcarolle, over accompaniments that use the three registers of the keyboard. Base the improvisations on the I-V-V-I harmonic phrase of the Schubert Waltz. Here are some possible beginnings:

EXERCISE 14: Improvising in Extended Forms on a Simple Harmonic Pattern

Dance forms of the Baroque period as in the sarabande (Example 1 below) or the minuet (Example 2 below) lend themselves to tonic-dominant improvisations. Note that the harmonic intervals in the minuet are primarily thirds and sixths. These harmonic intervals are the basic ones used in simple counterpoint.

a. Complete the examples below, and improvise other Baroque dances, such as the pavane, the

simple form of the courante , the gavotte, and the bourrée:

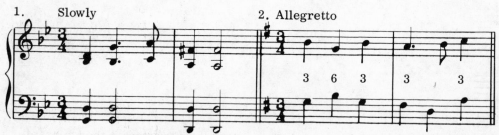

b. Longer forms can be improvised, still using the simple I-V harmonic patterns related to that of the Schubert Waltz. The original Schubert eight-measure pattern can be extended, through repetition, to become sixteen measures; these sixteen measures, in turn, can be repeated.

A large three-part or ternary form can be made by using the original eight-, sixteen-, or thirty-two-measure improvisation as Part I; moving to another key where the same harmonic pattern and the same musical style might be used, for Part II; then returning, for Part III, to the original key and a repetition of the musical material with which the improvisation started. Sample tonality forms might be as follows:

Part I (A)	Part II (B)	Part III (A)
G major	D major	G major
G major	E minor	G major
G minor	B♭ major	G minor

Improvise several large forms, basing the improvisations on any of the previous musical ideas, or on new ones.

THE SUB-DOMINANT HARMONY

The **sub-dominant** chord is the triad built on the fourth scale tone. It consists of scale degrees 4-6-8. In a major key it is a major triad (IV):

In minor, the sub-dominant triad is minor (iv):

EXERCISE 15: Finding and Using the Sub-Dominant Harmony

a. Find and play the sub-dominant chord in the keys of A, E^b, G minor, $C^\sharp$ minor, G^b, E, and A^b minor.

b. Analyze the spacing, voice progression, and doubling in the following I-IV-I and i-iv-i progressions. Transpose each example to at least six other keys:

c. Before 1600 and after the middle 1800's, tonality was often defined by the tonic and the sub-dominant, as in these examples:

1. Morales: *Magnificat Octavi Toni*

From *Treasury of Early Music*, Carl Parrish, 1954. Copyright © 1958 by W. W. Norton & Company, Inc., and used by permission.

2. Chopin: Mazurka, Opus 7, No. 3

d. Invent pianistic figures or short études based on the I-IV-I or i-iv-i progression as in the examples below. Each chord might be drawn out for several measures:

1.

2.

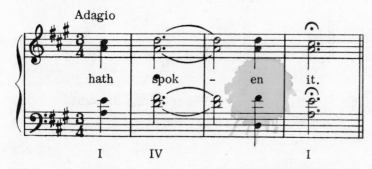

EXERCISE 16: The Plagal Cadence

In the **plagal cadence** the sub-dominant, with root in the bass, moves to a tonic, also with the root in the bass:

1. Handel: *Messiah*

2. Wagner: *Lohengrin*

The plagal cadence is sometimes called an "Amen" cadence since it comes at the end of almost every hymn, accompanying the word "Amen."

a. Play plagal cadences in the keys indicated by the key signatures. *Remember that each signature stands for a major and a minor key:*

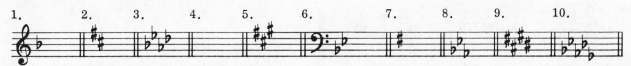

b. Play a descending major scale, from 8 to 1; add a plagal cadence, as shown below. Use each tone of the sub-dominant successively as a melody tone in the cadence. Repeat the exercise in at least four major and four minor keys. Any form of the minor may be used:

c. Construct plagal cadences, using the given bass tone as the root of a sub-dominant triad. (The min. below the tone signifies a minor sub-dominant.)

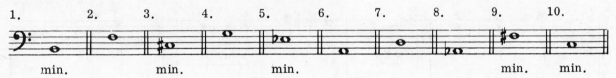

EXERCISE 17: Pre-Cadential Sub-Dominant Progressions

When used in first inversion, the sub-dominant moves smoothly to the tonic $\frac{6}{4}$ which in turn moves naturally to the V or the V^7. Note that in the I_4^6 either the fifth or the root of the chord is doubled; the same is true of the IV_4^6. The IV_4^6-I_4^6-V-I progression makes a strong final cadence.

a. Play and analyze the examples below. Then transpose each one to at least three other keys:

b. The IV_6 can move to destinations other than I_6^4. Like any chord, it can move to another of its own positions:

    IV6   IV

The IV_6 can also move to the V^7, a progression made easier from the viewpoint of voice leading because of the tone in common:

Play the two examples given above in minor as well as in major. Then transpose each to five other keys.

c. The IV in root position also moves easily to the I_6^4. Here are two sequences using this progression in alternating major and minor keys. Analyze the beginning of each sequence; then play each until the original opening key is reached:

1. Maximov

2.

d. The progression from IV to V, with both chords in root position, is one that composers have treated with care in order to avoid parallel motion in all voices. The best simple rule is to try to have all the upper voices move in contrary motion to the bass. Play and analyze the examples below, and transpose them to at least six other keys:

e. The IV in second inversion often occurs between two tonic chords. Play and analyze this example in which each tone of the IV appears in the soprano with an authentic cadence added on. Transpose the example to the keys of D minor, B^b, E, F minor, $C^\sharp$, and A^b minor:

f. Use all of the material suggested in the examples of this exercise in improvisation. Make each chord last for at least an entire measure. No. 1 in exercise a., for example, might be expanded to become:

EXERCISE 18: Improvising on the I-IV-V Harmonies of an Excerpt
from Schumann's *Faschingsschwank aus Wien*

a. Play and analyze the following four-measure phrase of Schumann's *Faschingsschwank aus Wien*. Note that its first two measures have a question-like quality, answered by the second two measures:

b. Play the harmonic plan of the Schumann in block chords. Then play it in piano figurations, so that the fingers feel the progression.

c. Use the harmonic plan of the Schumann in improvisations, doubling the time span given to each chord so that there are two phrases, each four measures in length: I-I-IV-I   I-I-V^7-I. Follow the plan used earlier in improvising on the harmonic plan of the Schubert Waltz. Make melodies that use chord and non-chord tones; change the meter from 2/4 to 3/4, 4/4, and 6/8; change the mode to minor, etc. The following examples show two possible beginnings. Finish them and invent at least six others:

d. The harmonic plan can be put into a left-hand form that lies easily under the hand: put the IV into its 6 position, and the V or the V^7 into its first inversion:

This variant of the original pattern lends itself to becoming a simple waltz:

Or, by changing the accompaniment to an Alberti bass, it can suggest Mozart:

e. When the chords of this pattern are put into an open position, and the mode changed to minor, the left-hand part can become the accompaniment for an *Allegro appassionato* (No. 1 below) or a tango (No. 2):

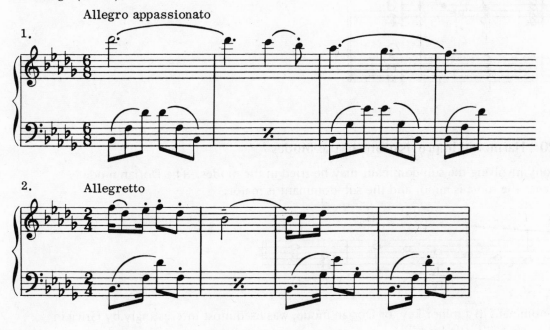

EXERCISE 19: Altering the Mode of the Sub-Dominant

Composers sometimes play fast and loose with the mode of the sub-dominant, often making the chord minor in the major mode. Wagner was especially fond of using a minor sub-dominant-tonic progression as the final cadence of an opera. (See the endings of *Tristan und Isolde*, *Die Meistersinger*, and *Götterdämmerung*.) Play and analyze the following examples; transpose each example to at least three other keys:

1. Chopin: Mazurka, Opus 50, No. 1

2. MacDowell: *Sea Pieces*

3. Chopin: Nocturne, Opus 32, No. 2

EXERCISE 20: Harmonic Improvisations in the Modes

Diatonic harmony involving the sub-dominant may be tried in the modes. The Dorian mode is interesting because the tonic is minor and the sub-dominant is major:

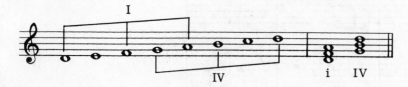

The major sub-dominant in a minor key, or Dorian mode, was used most interestingly by Grieg in his piano piece *Voglein* ("Little Bird"):

Improvise short pieces in the modes, using only tonic and sub-dominant harmonies. The following example shows one possible beginning (the sign 𝄎 is another way of indicating a two-measure repeat):

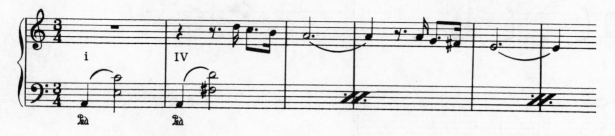

EXERCISE 21: Further Improvisations Using the Tonic, Sub-Dominant, and Dominant

a. Following the principle of the exercises dealing with improvisations based on the short pieces by Schubert and Schumann, improvise, in pianistic style and in four-voice hymn style, short pieces based on these harmonic progressions:

1. A major: I-I-I-V   I-IV-V-I

2. E minor: i-V-i-V   i-i6₄-V-I

3. D♭ major: I-I-I-V   V-V-V-I

4. G minor: i-iv-i-iv   i-iv-i-V-i

5. E♭ major: I-IV-I-V   I-IV-V-I

6. C minor:

      i   V⁴₃   i6   iv   i6 V⁴₃ i   V   i   V⁴₃ i6   i   iv V7   i

7. Figured basses:

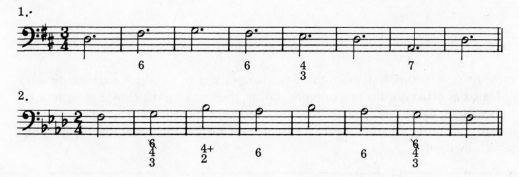

b. Make harmonic phrases that use I, IV, and V⁷, and improvise folksong-like melodies based on the harmonic progressions. Note that while the IV usually moves to I, it can also progress to V or V⁷; the V, which usually progresses to I, can move to IV. In at least one improvisation substitute a minor iv for a major IV in a major key.

c. The Schubert and Schumann examples, on which earlier improvisations were based, were composed in symmetrical two- and four-measure phrases. Many folk songs and popular songs, however, are built in three- and five-measure phrases. Be sure to include some non-symmetrical phrases in the improvisations, such as:

3/4:   I | I₆ | V | I | I₆ | IV | I   or

6/8:   i | V | i | i₆ | iv | V | i | i₆ | iv-V⁷ | i

11

HARMONIZING MELODIES WITH I, IV, AND V OR V⁷

Choosing an Accompaniment Style; Playing Melodies by Ear; Harmonizing Melodies

Harmonizing a melody is, at its simplest, discovering the harmonic plan on which the melody was based originally. Melodies often outline one or more chords, thus making the choice of harmony quite easy. If, for example, we did not already have the accompaniment for the Schubert Waltz quoted in the preceding chapter, we could easily harmonize the melody by extracting the harmonic scheme from the melody itself:

Note that each chord lasts for at least one complete measure. The harmonic rhythm—the rate of chord change—of the Waltz is moderately slow. In a fast harmonic rhythm, found in many step-wise chorale melodies, chords change on every beat.

EXERCISE 1: Harmonizing Simple Melodies

a. Using simple chords in the left hand, play the harmonies outlined by the melodies below:

1. "Skip to My Lou" (American)

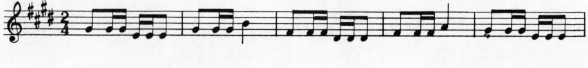

166

2. "The Keel Row" (Scottish)

3. "Lolotte" (American Creole)

4. Schubert: "Das Wandern"

5. Mozart: *Don Giovanni*

b. When harmonizing a melody, it is always important to analyze its form in detail. First determine the beginnings and endings of phrases; then decide what chords might be used at cadence points. In this Mozart example there is a cadence, or feeling of momentary pause, in the fourth measure. This type of cadence, indicating a pause but not a complete stop, is known as a **half-cadence** or **semi-cadence**. Any chord may be used at a semi-cadence; in the Mozart, a dominant chord seems expected:

Mozart: Symphony No. 39

Play the cadence chords of the following melodies:

1. "Silent Night"

2. "Oh, Susannah"

3. "London Bridge"

4. "Sur le Pont d'Avignon"

c. Melodies often are built of combinations of chords and scales. While a chord-line melody gives an indication of the harmony, a scale-line melody, which moves by step, does not. In the Beethoven Dance below, the first two measures seem to outline a tonic triad. The scale-line melody of measures 3 and 4 does not suggest a chord; it would be possible to harmonize these measures with various combinations of primary chords—I, IV, and V. Try several possibilities before making a final choice. Only the player's ear and sensitivity, plus his experience, can ultimately determine which chords to use:

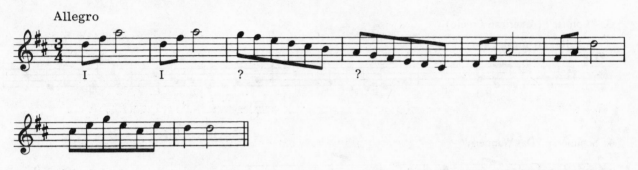

Play a simple harmonic accompaniment to the Beethoven Dance, and to the following melodies, all of which combine chord tones and scale-wise motion:

1. "Lavender's Blue" (English)

2. Schubert: "Der Lindenbaum"

3. "Dame, Get Up and Bake Your Pies" (English)

Allegro

G min.:

d. Melodies that move by step—as in many chorales or hymn tunes—pose problems of chord choice, inversions, and voice leading. The chorale tune "O Ewigkeit du Donnerwort" illustrates some of these problems:

An analysis of the melody shows that it can be broken into four different small units, as marked in the example above. Each unit has several possible harmonizations, as shown below. Practice the various harmonizations in at least six other major and minor keys:

Scale degrees 1-2-3 or 3-2-1

Scale degrees 3-4-5 or 5-4-3

Scale degrees 5-6-7-8

Scale degrees 5-4-3-2

One possible harmonization of the chorale phrases might be this:

Make several other harmonizations of this chorale.

e. Short melodic units that are found in music can be harmonized as shown below. Play and analyze these examples, and transpose them to at least six other major and minor keys:

Scale degrees 1-7-1   Scale degrees 5-7-8   Scale degrees 1-6-5

Scale degrees 3-7-1

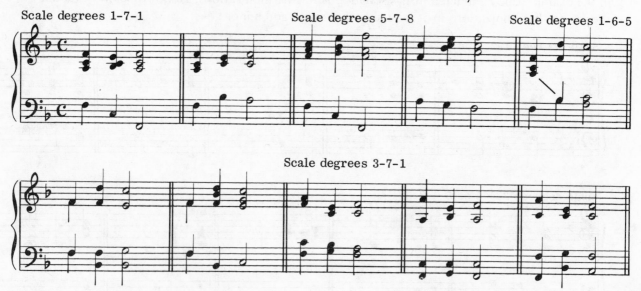

f. Using some of the above suggestions, play simple harmonic accompaniments, using the three primary chords, for these melodies. Note that their motion is primarily step-wise:

1. "Hastings" (hymn tune)

2. "Der Flug der Liebe" (German)

3. "Es Kostet viel, ein Christ zu sein"

4. "Seelen – Bräutigam"

g. Many melodies consist of principal tones decorated with neighboring tones, appoggiaturas, and passing tones. In harmonizing such melodies, first reduce them to their skeletal forms, eliminating the decorating tones. Then harmonize the principal tones, as in this example:

"Come Let Us Be Joyful" (German)

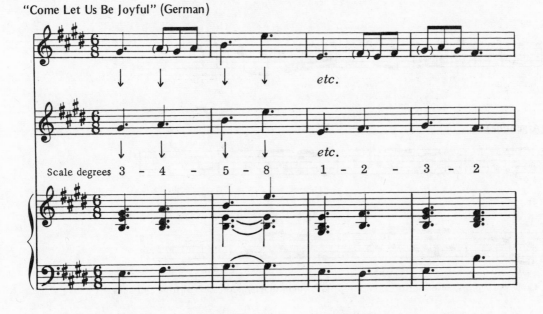

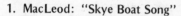

Play simple harmonic accompaniments, not necessarily in chorale style, for these melodies that consist of principal tones and decorating tones:

1. MacLeod: "Skye Boat Song"

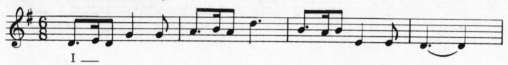

2. Mozart: Piano Sonata, K. 309

Allegretto grazioso

3. "La Vidalita" (Argentine)

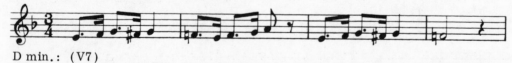

From Irma Labastille, *Canciones Tipicas*, Silver Burdett Company, 1941. Reprinted by permission of Irma Labastille.

4. Beethoven: Six Variations for Piano on Paisiello's "Nel cor piu non mi sento"

h. In some melodies, the principal harmonic tone is preceded on a strong beat by a sounded or held suspension or appoggiatura. In the following Schubert Dance, the F in the second measure is harmonized with the dominant, even though it is part of the chord of the preceding measure. Once a pattern like this has been established, it will probably recur in subsequent measures:

Schubert: Ländler

i. The following melodies have disguised principal tones. Put simple harmonic accompaniments to them, trying several approaches:

1. Tchaikovsky: *Swan Lake*

2. Schubert: "Was ist Sylvia?"

3. "Dark Eyes" (Russian)

i6 _____ iv _____ i6 _____

V$\frac{4}{3}$ _____ V7 _____ i _____

j. The use of suspensions is so prevalent in music—with one tone, two tones, or even entire chords suspended—that this short exercise should become thoroughly familiar to the player's fingers. Analyze the eight-measure unit and play it in the major and minor keys of F, G, E, A^b, B^b, D, and G^b (F$\sharp$). Then practice it as broken chords, as in the variant suggested:

Variant

k. The first, fourth, and fifth tones of the scale each belong to two primary chords: 1 to I and IV; 4 to IV and V; 5 to I and V:

C Maj.:   I – IV   IV – V7   V – I

When one of these tones is an important melodic tone, the player must make a choice. This choice is determined by context, and by the player's ear after he has tried the several possibilities. *Remember, there is no one way to harmonize any melody.* Try several versions. Look for fresh and even unusual ways to harmonize a melody. Personal preference and taste is the ultimate judge. Play simple harmonic accompaniments to the following melodies. Each of them contains one or more places that can be harmonized in more than one way:

1. "Clementine" (American)

2. Schubert: "Wohin?"

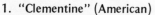

3. Sullivan: "Onward Christian Soldiers"

I. Many melodies begin with scale degrees 3-2-1, with the first two notes as **upbeats**. These tones are usually harmonized with a dominant, as in "The First Noel":

(This form of the dominant is sometimes referred to as the dominant thirteenth.)

Harmonize in similar fashion these beginnings:

1. "Believe Me, If All These Endearing Young Charms" (Irish)

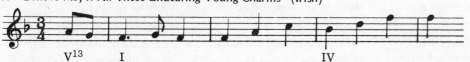

2. "Annie Laurie" (Scottish)   3. Foster: "Gentle Annie"

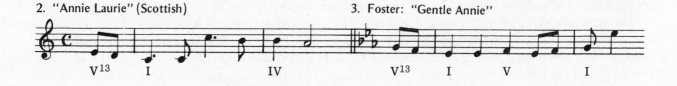

The unit consisting of scale degrees 2-3-1 is often found at a cadence point. In most cases the harmony is obviously a V^7 moving to a I, with scale degree 3 serving as a kind of decoration of scale degree 2:

"Spiritual Tune"

Make a simple harmonic accompaniment to this melody by Rousseau in which there are 2-3-1 melodic cadences:

Rousseau: "Lullaby"

CHOOSING AN ACCOMPANIMENT STYLE

There is no one "correct" accompaniment style for any given melody. Much depends upon the type of melody to be harmonized. Schubert, in his songs, chose his accompaniments carefully, providing not only an harmonic background for the melody, but a dramatic underlining of the text. "The Erlking," for instance, has a driving, rushing piano part, while the accompaniment to "The Hedge Rose" is as simple as the melody and text. Most heart-rending is the austere drone bass that establishes the tired, plodding quality of "The Organ Grinder," from his song cycle *Die Winterreise*.

Tempo, mood, and melodic activity (or its absence) influence the type of accompaniment. So too does the circumstance for which the accompaniment will be used. Someone playing for his own amusement might see how inventive his accompaniment could be, while someone playing for group singing would try to make the music as clear and full as possible.

Some of the principal accompaniment styles are illustrated on the following pages. They are taken, for the most part, from arrangements the authors have made for *The Fireside Book of Folksongs* (Simon & Schuster), *The Fireside Book of Favorite American Songs* (Simon & Schuster), and *The American Heritage Songbook* (American Heritage). The student is urged to start a notebook of accompaniment styles as he comes across them in music.

EXERCISE 2: A Catalog of Accompaniment Styles

a. Simplest of all accompaniments, although not necessarily the easiest, is the four-part hymn or
chorale style, in which the melody seems to be arranged for soprano, alto, tenor, and bass voices.
The four-part style is particularly useful for harmonizing melodies which move, for the most part,
in step-wise fashion, and which imply a fast harmonic rhythm. Not all hymns or church pieces,
however, change chords with every beat, as these two examples show. Continue each harmonization in a style consistent with that established at the beginning. Note that No. 2, "Silent Night,"
employs duets paralleling the melody at the interval of the third or the sixth:

1. "Greenfields" (hymn tune)

2. Gruber: "Silent Night"

b. Another useful style of accompaniment is that which suggests a guitar, either by using full chords under the melody, or by dividing the chord tones into broken chords or arpeggios:

1. "Bold Brennan on the Moor" (Irish)

2. "I Am a Poor Wayfarin' Stranger" (American)

3. "Hatikvah" (Israeli)

4. "Captain Kidd" (American)

c. With an active melody, an ostinato pattern or drone bass can be effective. Chord tones can be added, sparingly or not at all, in the right hand, under the melody:

1. "Scarborough Fair" (English)

2. "Comin' Round the Mountain" (American)

3. "The Irish Washerwoman"

d. One of the most useful styles of accompaniment is the "swing" or "oom-pah" bass. As its name implies, it is an accompaniment in which the left hand swings back and forth from single tones in the bass register to the chord in the middle register. The bass tone is usually the root or fifth of the chord, although it may be the third:

The Hutchinson Family: "Uncle Sam's Farm"

e. The melody can be played in the left hand, with chords played in the middle register by the right hand:

1. Foster: "Oh, Susannah"

2. "Blow the Man Down" (chantey)

f. The Alberti bass is a simple style of accompaniment that lies well under the hand. It can be modified by mixing it with other types of accompaniment, including little duets in thirds and sixths between the melody and other voices:

1. Mozart: *The Abduction from the Seraglio*

2. Mozart: *Don Giovanni*

Andante grazioso

g. Open positions of chords provide a resonant accompaniment to lyric melodies:

1. "The Pesky Sarpent" (American)

2. "The Quilting Party" (American)

h. Chord tones can be played under the melody in the right hand as the left hand plays only the bass notes:

1. "Down in the Valley" (American)

2. "Red River Valley" (American)

i. For accompanying large-group singing, the melody can be played in octaves, with chord tones filled in, in the right hand, on accents. With this, the left hand usually plays some form of swing bass:

"Alouette" (French Canadian)

j. Most musical of all is the kind of accompaniment that adds a dramatic dimension to the melody by illustrating the text. The best way to understand how this can happen is to study Schubert's songs. A simple melody such as:

becomes transformed when Schubert adds the whirring suggestion of a spinning wheel:

Schubert: "Gretchen am Spinnrad"

(Here the melody itself no longer appears as the top line of the piano part. Schubert assumes that someone will sing the melody while the pianist's two hands are both busy with the accompaniment.) The dramatic accompaniment usually depends upon the use of one or more melodic-rhythmic figures that have a certain symbolism for the composer and, he hopes, for his listeners. (It is neither possible nor necessary to find a dramatic accompaniment for every melody.)   In this cowboy song, the left hand suggests, to some extent, the sound and feel of cantering hoofbeats:

"Ol' Texas" (American)

k. The melodies that follow can all be harmonized with the three primary chords. Try them with various styles of accompaniment:

1. "Can't You Dance the Polka?" (chantey)

2. Mason: "There Is a Fountain"

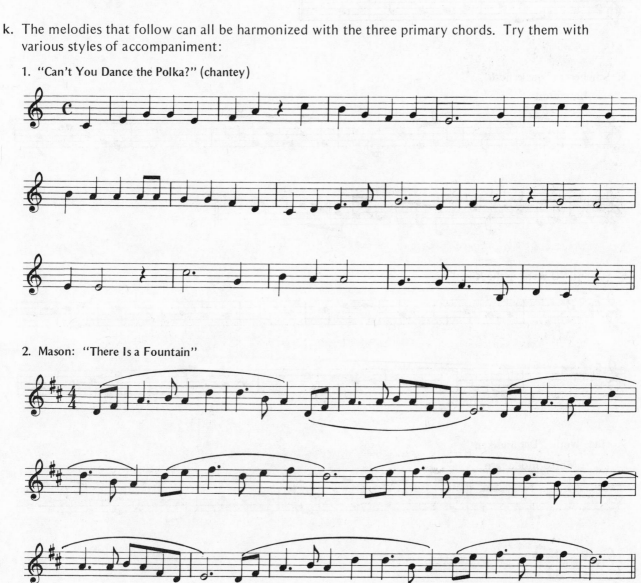

3. Marsh: "Jesus, Lover of My Soul"

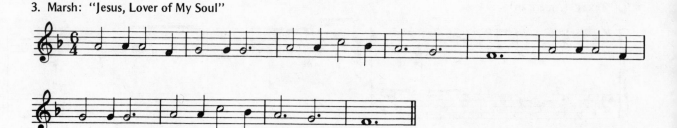

4. Handel: "Sarabande"

iv6 iv   i

V

5. Schubert: "Wasserfluth"

Langsam

6. Haydn: "O Worship the King"

7. Hugo Wolf: "Der Musikant"

Molto moderato

8. French Carol

E min.: i   IV

9. Mazas: Opus 36

Andante

E min.: ⸓   i

10. Mazas: Opus 36

Allegro moderato

PLAYING MELODIES BY EAR; HARMONIZING MELODIES

Musicians are often expected to be able to play melodies on their instruments without having access to printed copies of the music. Keyboard players are further expected to improvise accompaniments for such melodies.

Playing music without reference to a score is known as "playing by ear." Playing by ear is a natural gift for some fortunate ones; but it is also a skill that can be developed by thoughtful exploration and practice. It is also a skill that develops through trial and error. The player must be undaunted by his mistakes, and be able to learn from them.

Playing by ear depends a great deal on memory: unless the player can remember the melody, there is no way he can pick out its tones on the keyboard. Also, the more melodies one knows and tries to play by ear, the more one should become aware of how melodic, rhythmic, and harmonic formulas keep recurring.

EXERCISE 3: Finding the Keynote and Scale of a Melody

a. Decide on a simple tune to be played by ear, such as "Twinkle, Twinkle, Little Star" ("Ah, vous dirais-je, Maman"). Select and play a tone on the piano as the starting pitch for the song. Sing through the song and check the ending tone against the starting tone. In this song, the starting and ending tones are the same. Since most songs end on the tonic of the scale in which the melody is composed, it can be assumed that "Twinkle, Twinkle" begins and ends on the keynote, or tonic. *(The majority of familiar songs start on the tonic, fifth degree, or third degree of the scale—in that order of frequency.)*

Sing at least twenty familiar melodies, determining the starting scale degree of each.

b. The relationship between the first and second pitches of the melody often gives a hint as to the scale degree of the starting tone:

1. When the melody starts with the leap of a perfect fourth *upward*, the upper tone is usually the tonic: "O Tannenbaum," "Santa Lucia," "Hark! the Herald Angels Sing," "Down in the Valley," "Blue Room," "The Marseillaise," etc.

2. The leap of a perfect fourth *downward* suggests that the first tone is probably the keynote: "Clementine," "Adeste Fidelis," "Gaudeamus Igitur," etc.

3. When the melody moves *upward* from the starting tone other than by the leap of a perfect fourth, the probability is that the first tone is the keynote: "Oh, Susannah," "Au Clair de la Lune," "Sweet Betsey from Pike," "On Top of Old Smokey," etc.

   However, if the first several tones fill in the interval of a perfect fourth, the starting tone might be the fifth scale degree: "Chester," "I'm Gonna Wash that Man Right Out of My Hair," "She'll Be Coming 'Round the Mountain," etc.

4. When the melody moves *downward* from the starting tone other than by a leap of a perfect fourth, the starting tone is probably the third or fifth scale degree (except for melodies that go down the scale from 8 to 1, as, for instance, "Joy to the World"): "Deck the Halls," "The Star-Spangled Banner," "The First Noel," "Night and Day," "Merrily We Roll Along," etc.

c. Having decided on the keynote, the next step is to discover whether the scale is major, minor, or, as in the case of many folk songs, modal. The principal tone to consider is the third degree of the scale. Test its mode by playing the keynote plus the major third above the keynote in the left hand while playing the melody with the right hand. If there is a clash, try the minor third above the keynote.

d. Once the starting tone and the type of scale have been established, the melody must be examined —by ear. Look for small units, such as a group of tones that outline a chord (particularly the I, IV, or V⁷) or form part of a scale:

1. Chord outlines: "Clementine," "On Top of Old Smokey," etc.

2. Scale forms: "America," "Au Clair de la Lune," "Joy to the World," etc.

Look also for repetitions and sequences: "America" (2nd part), "Yankee Doodle" (2nd part), "Tea for Two," "My Funny Valentine," "Never on Sunday," etc.

Within a repetition or sequence, the size of one interval might change so that it becomes successively larger ("Blue Room") or successively smaller ("Over the Rainbow").

EXERCISE 4: Finding the Meter of a Melody

In deciding on the meter of a melody, it is important to ascertain whether it begins on a stressed tone ("on the downbeat") or on an unstressed tone ("on the upbeat"). The chances are that successive phrases will continue the style of the beginning of the melody, just as a poem that starts in iambics will continue in iambics, and not suddenly switch to trochees.

a. Sing or play the opening tones of the songs suggested above. If the words are known, say them aloud. Decide whether the first word is stressed ("DECK the halls . . . ," "TWINKLE, twinkle . . .") or unstressed ("Oh, say can you SEE . . . ," "The FIRST Noel . . . ").

b. Play or sing the melody, meanwhile tapping the foot in a steady beat or playing a steady drum beat deep in the bass with the left hand. Feel where a regular emphasis or accent keeps recurring. Decide whether that accent—the measure accent—comes every two or every three beats. Play the melody with the right hand while the left hand plays a drone bass on the accent. It is often difficult to distinguish between a meter of two and a meter of four. "Twinkle, Twinkle" is obviously in a meter of two whereas "Au clair de la lune" could be in a meter of two or four:

```
Au clair de la lun-e
 1   2   3  4   1
 1   +   2  +   1
```

When beats seem to be divided into groupings of three, the meter could be compound: 6, 9, or 12.

EXERCISE 5: Ear Training

a. Play by ear as many melodies as you can remember: folk tunes, popular songs, themes from concert and operatic works. Practice this form of ear training by visualizing mentally the notation of the music as you listen.

b. The following well-known melodies can be harmonized with primary triads, although all will not use the IV harmony. Play the melodies by ear and harmonize them with chords or a simple accompaniment pattern in the left hand. The keys suggested will put each song in a good vocal range:

1. "Three Blind Mice" *(key of D)*
2. "Dixie" (verse only) *(key of C)*
3. Brahms' "Lullaby" *(Eᵇ)*
4. "Ach du lieber Augustine" ("Did You Ever See a Lassie?") *(A)*
5. "Careless Love" *(Eᵇ)*
6. "St. Louis Blues" (chorus) *(G)*
7. "The Arkansas Traveler" *(F)*
8. "Turkey in the Straw" *(G)*
9. "Green Grow the Lilacs" *(G)*
10. "Old Abe Lincoln" ("The Old Grey Mare") *(A)*
11. "Tenting Tonight" *(G)*

12. "Listen to the Mocking Bird" *(F)*
13. "The Old Oaken Bucket" *(G)*
14. "Little Brown Jug" *(A)*
15. "The Wearin' of the Green" *(D)*
16. "For the Beauty of the Earth" *(G)*
17. "Blest Be the Tie That Binds" *(F)*

18. "Just As I Am Without One Plea" *(E♭)*
19. "Rock of Ages" *(B♭)*
20. "O Happy Day" *(G)*
21. "He Leadeth Me" *(D)*
22. "Sweet Hour of Prayer" *(D)*

12
THE SUPER-TONIC HARMONIES

The tonic, dominant, and sub-dominant harmonies are often referred to as the **primary chords** in a key. Entire short compositions can be made with these chords, or even with only two of them. The chords built on other diatonic scale tones are termed **secondary chords**, since they are used in a more limited fashion. Without these chords, and without chromatic chords, however, much of the music of the eighteenth and nineteenth centuries could not have been written. The **super-tonic** chord is built on the second degree of the diatonic scale, and consists of scale degrees 2, 4, and 6.

EXERCISE 1: Building and Playing Super-Tonics in Major and Minor

a. Play the ascending scale of C major, followed by the triad built on the second scale degree, in this rhythmic fashion:

Note that in a major scale, the super-tonic triad is a minor chord, indicated as ii. Repeat the above exercise in the keys of E^b, A, D^b, B, A^b, and F$^\sharp$.

b. Play the descending scale of A natural minor, followed by the three positions of the super-tonic in that key, in this rhythmic pattern:

In the natural and harmonic minor scales, the super-tonic triad is a diminished triad, indicated as ii$^\circ$. Repeat the example in the natural minor keys of D, C, E, B^b, F$^\sharp$, and E^b.

EXERCISE 2: Progression of the Super-Tonic

The super-tonic has a dominant relationship to the dominant (V) and usually progresses to it. The V, in turn, resolves to the I, making a small segment of the circle of fifths:

ii ___ V ___ I

a. Consider each of the given bass tones to be the root of a ii in a major key. Play the triad in the right hand, after playing the bass tone in the left, and progress to the correct V^7 and I, as in the example:

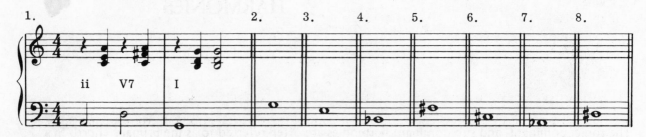

b. Think of each of the following bass tones as the root of a super-tonic triad in a minor key. With the right hand play the correct triad above the bass tone; resolve the chord to the proper V^7 and i, as shown in the example under a. above:

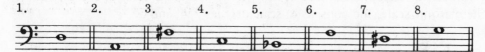

c. Continue the following sequential patterns until the starting chord is reached again:

1.

2.

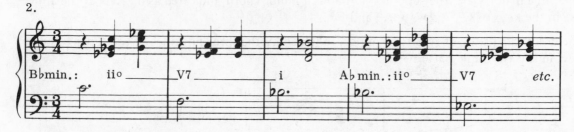

d. Play a descending major scale, from 8 to 1. Add to it the following melodic cadences: 2-7-1; 4-4-3; 6-5-5; 6-7-8. Harmonize the cadence tones with ii-V-I as shown in this example:

Repeat this exercise in the major keys of B^b, E^b, A, F, C$^\sharp$, B, and A^b.

e. The above exercise may be played in minor, using the descending natural minor scale, *but using the triads from the harmonic form of the minor scale* and making the last melodic cadence 6-5-8 as shown below:

Repeat the above exercise in the minor keys of A, D, F, C, B, E, B^b, and F$^\sharp$.

f. Play the super-tonic which precedes each of the following dominant sevenths. Resolve each dominant to a major or minor tonic. Move the voices as smoothly as possible, trying to achieve contrary motion, particularly between the outer voices:

g. Expand the following fragments, and improvise other etudes, lyrical pieces, and dances based on the chord progression I-ii-V⁷-I:

In this example, the functions of the hands can be reversed after one or two phrases, putting the chords in the left hand and the rhythmic pattern in the right:

In this étude, chord tones are preceded by lower neighboring tones:

Appoggiaturas are the main ingredients in this waltz melody:

h. The super-tonic is often used in its first inversion. In this position, the third of the chord—the bass tone—is usually doubled:

1. Mozart: *Don Giovanni*

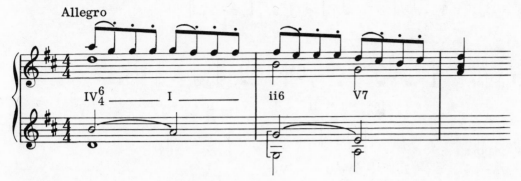

2. Bach: Chorale, "Gib dich zufrieden und sei stille"

In the Bach chorale above, the ii°6 moves to a i6; this is a common cadential progression, one which usually occurs when the melodic line moves downward 4-3-2-1:

Analyze the example above, and transpose it to at least six other major or minor keys.

i. In moving from the ii6 or the ii°6, with doubled third, to the V7, try to keep one tone in common. Transpose the following progressions to three major and three minor keys:

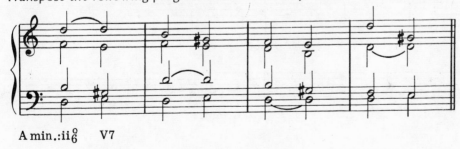

A min.: ii°6   V7

j. Play the indicated harmonies and rhythmic pattern in the given keys. The realization can be done in a four-voice chorale style or freely:

1. D minor; B minor:
   i   ii°$_6$ —— i$_4^6$ V7   i

2. F major; C♯ major:
   I   I6   IV   ii   I$_4^6$ V7 —— I

3. D major; A♭ major:
   I   IV6   ii6   V7 ——   I

4. E♭ minor; F♯ minor:
   ii°$_6$ V   V$_2^4$ i6

5. B major; E♭ major:
   I6   I   IV   IV6   ii6   V$_3^4$ V7   I

k. Add three upper voices to the following figured basses:

1.
   6   6 ——   6

2.
   6   6   6$_4$ 7

3.
   6   6   6$_4$ —— 7

4.
   4$_2$ 6   6   6   4$_3$

1. Harmonize the following melodic fragments, which might be beginnings or endings of phrases, using the super-tonic triad in appropriate places. (In the first three fragments, an asterisk (*) shows where it might be used.)

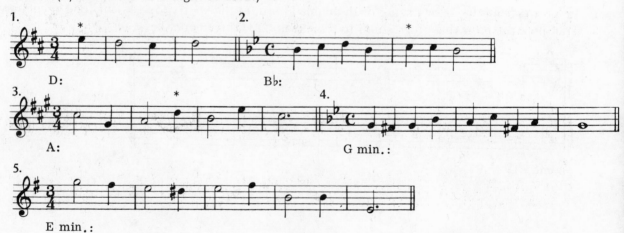

1.   *
D:

2.   *
B♭:

3.   *
A:

4.
G min.:

5.
E min.:

EXERCISE 3: The Super-Tonic Seventh

The super-tonic harmony often includes a seventh. In major keys, the super-tonic seventh is a minor seventh (ii^7):

C:

In minor keys, the super-tonic seventh is a half-diminished seventh ($ii^{\varnothing 7}$):

C min.:

a. Play all positions of the diatonic super-tonic sevenths in the keys of D, G minor, E, B^b minor, D^b, and D minor, as in this example:

C: $ii7$ ii^6_5 ii^4_3 ii^4_2

b. The super-tonic seventh, like the super-tonic triad, resolves most often to the dominant seventh, the dominant, or the tonic 6. Analyze each of the following examples; play it in minor as well as in major. Transpose each to three major and three minor keys. Note that the super-tonic seventh is treated in the same way in minor as in major:

3.

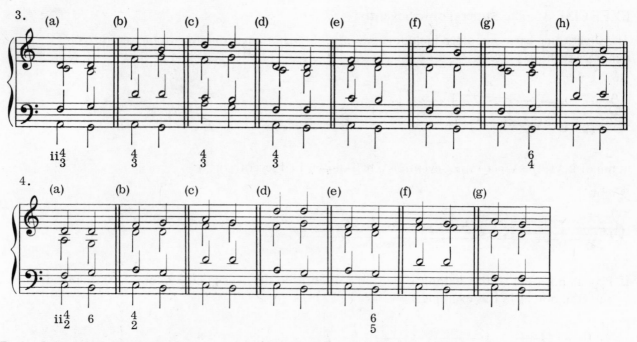

4.

c. Each of the following chords is to be considered a super-tonic seventh. Resolve each to a logical V, V^7 or I$_6^4$:

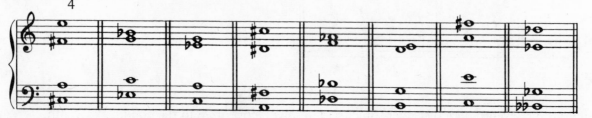

d. Each of the given bass notes is to be treated as the root, third, fifth, and seventh of a ii^7 and a ii$^{\circ7}$. Fill in the other tones of the chord with proper spacing and resolve each chord to a V, V^7 or I$_6^4$:

e. Continue the following sequences until the starting chord is reached again:

1.

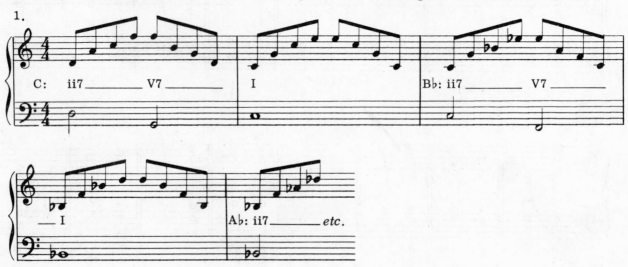

Try decorating each sequence. This example shows a possible variation of No. 4:

f. Super-tonic sevenths are often to be found at cadence points, particularly when the melodic line is basically 3-2-1, or simply 2-1. Analyze the following cadences, drawn from Bach chorale harmonizations, and transpose each cadence to at least four other keys:

g. Realize the following figured basses:

1.

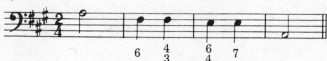

2.   3.

4.

h. Many composers use the super-tonic seventh in the opening phrases of their works as well as for cadence purposes. The following examples from music literature are to be analyzed and transposed to at least three other keys:

1. Schumann: "Ich will meine Seele tauchen"

Leise

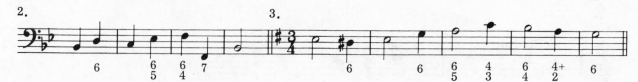

etc.

2. Mozart: Piano Sonata, K. 280

etc.

3. Tchaikovsky: "In Early Spring"

etc.

4. Bach: *Well-Tempered Clavier*

5. Bach: *Well-Tempered Clavier*

i. In the following examples, the opening patterns have been reduced to their **block harmonies**, that is, the music reduced to its basic harmonic plan, ignoring all non-harmonic tones:

1. Mendelssohn: *Songs Without Words*

2. Bach: *Well-Tempered Clavier*

Look at the openings of other musical works, seeing how many use a super-tonic or super-tonic seventh in the opening phrases, and play these phrases in block harmony.

j. Improvise several short motives, basing each on the outline of a tonic chord, but including passing and neighboring tones. Spin each motive over the harmonic phrases used in the Bach and Mendelssohn examples above.

k. Improvise on the harmonic phrases of the Bach and Mendelssohn above an étude, a waltz, a nocturne, and a song-like piece.

l. Expand the improvisations you have done on the Bach and Mendelssohn examples above into longer compositions by moving to a second section in a related key. In this section, use the harmonic plan as in the first section. Then return to the original key and repeat the first section. (Because these "compositions" are improvised, repetitions will not necessarily be exact; they should, however, be close to and reminiscent of the original phrase.)

ALTERED FORMS OF THE SUPER-TONIC SEVENTH

The super-tonic seventh is a volatile harmony; it does not always stay in its original diatonic form. The two most usual alterations of the super-tonic seventh are: borrowing of the minor form (ii°7) in a major key; changing the chord by raising its third (II7).

EXERCISE 4: Borrowing the Minor's Super-Tonic Seventh for the Major

The super-tonic seventh in its minor key form is a half-diminished seventh, that is, a diminished triad plus a major third:

While the borrowed ii°7 is found in all kinds of music, it probably has been used more by composers of the Romantic period:

1. Schumann: "Ich grolle nicht"
   Nicht zu schnell

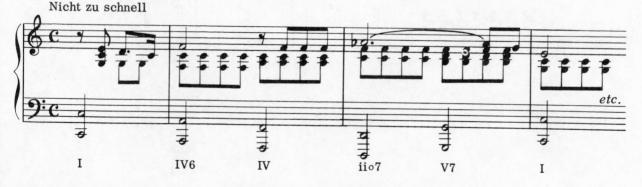

2. Tchaikovsky: "Pimpinella"

ii$_3^4$ ii°$_3^4$ V7   I

a. Play the following harmonic patterns in the major keys of E^b, A, F, and B. Play the patterns first as block chords, then as études, nocturnes, etc.:

1. I-I$_6$-ii$_6$-ii°^{7}-V-V^7-I

2. I-IV-I-ii°$_4$-I$_6$-V^7-I
           3 4

3. I-V$_4$-I$_6$-IV-ii°$_6$-I$_6$-V-V^7-I
      3   5 4

b. Realize these figured basses:

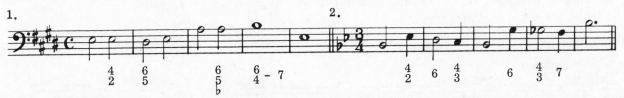

c. Harmonize the following melodic fragments, using a form of the borrowed super-tonic seventh at least once in each example:

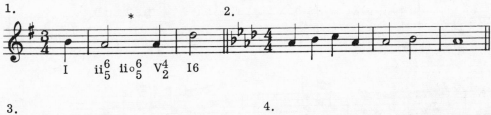

I   ii$_5^6$ ii°$_5^6$ V$_2^4$ I6

EXERCISE 5: Chromatic Alteration: Raising the Third of the Super-Tonic Seventh

The super-tonic seventh with a raised third (II^7) is one of the most common chromatic chords. In almost every case, the II^7 functions as the dominant of V:

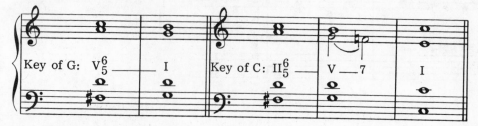

Play the progression II_6-V^7-I in the keys of D, F, A^b, B, and E^b, first in four-part harmony, as above, then in pianistic styles.[5]

EXERCISE 6: Improvising with Super-Tonic Seventh Progressions

Traditional harmony functions within a system analogous to our solar system. The tonic chord exerts a gravitational pull on the other diatonic chords, similar to the sun's pull on its planets. But, just as each planet can have its own satellites or moons, so too can a diatonic chord have its satellite dominants, super-tonics, etc. In this passage from Mozart's *Don Giovanni* there is a momentary use of a II^7 as the V^7 of V in measures 2 and 3:

Mozart: *Don Giovanni*

a. Reduce the Mozart example to block harmony; then improvise several short pieces based on its harmonic plan. Note how Mozart achieves interest: he balances a four-bar phrase with one of six bars; he avoids a cadence in measure 8 by using a I_6 rather than a I in root position; he uses the diatonic ii_6 in the second phrase instead of repeating the plan of measure 2. As an experiment, play the example, but jump from the end of measure 7 directly to measure 10: a lesser composer might have written the music that way.

b. The example below shows Beethoven's use of the II^7 in his Piano Sonata, Opus 109. Note the strong melodic bass; if only the outer voices are played, the result is an interesting two-part counterpoint. Transpose the example to the keys of F, G, and B^b:

c. The II⁷ preceding a V or a V⁷ is to be found in minor as well as in major keys, often at cadence points. Analyze the harmonies of the Bach cadences below, and transpose each example to three other minor keys:

d. Composers occasionally have used some form of the super-tonic seventh at the beginning of a work, as in Schumann's "Warum":

Invent opening phrases that use II⁷ and ii°⁷ as the opening chord.

e. Improvise short pieces based on the harmonic progressions outlined below. Each chord might receive only one or two beats, making a fast harmonic rhythm (although probably a slow tempo) and a short improvisation. Or, each chord might be stretched out over one or two measures. A good exercise is to see how long, by using embellishing tones, an harmonic sound can be prolonged without losing the basic sense of the chord:

1. A major: I-ii₆-I₆-V V⁷-I₆-ii-V⁷-I

2. G major: $\overset{\frown}{\text{I-IV}_6\text{-V}_6\text{-I-I}_6\text{IV-I}_6\text{-I-V}}$ | $\overset{\frown}{\text{I-V}_6\text{-I-V}_4^3\text{-I}_6\text{-ii}_6^5\text{-V}^7\text{-I}}$

3. D major: $\text{I-IV-I}_6\text{-IV}_6\text{-V}_6^5\text{-I-ii}_6^5\text{-V-I}$

4. F major: $\overset{\frown}{\text{I-I}_6\text{-IV-I}_6\text{-V}_4^2\text{-I}_6\text{-I-V}_6\text{-II}_4^3\text{-V}}$ | $\overset{\frown}{\text{V}_6^5\text{-I-IV-I}_6\text{-V}_4^3\text{-I-ii}_6^{\circ5}\text{-V}^7\text{-I}}$

5. D^b major: $\overset{\frown}{\text{V}^7\text{-I-I}_6\text{-IV-IV}_6\text{-V}_6^5\text{-I}}$ | $\overset{\frown}{\text{I}_6\text{-ii-ii}_6\text{-II}_6^5\text{-V}^7\text{-I}}$

6. C$^\sharp$ minor: $\text{i-V}_4^3\text{-V}_6^5\text{-i-i}_6\text{-II}^7\text{-V}^7\text{-i}$

7. E minor: $\text{V}_6^5\text{-i-V}_4^3\text{-i}_6\text{-ii}_6^{\circ5}\text{-i}_6^4\text{-V}^7\text{-i}$

f. Use these guitar symbols as bases for improvisations:

1. Amin/E7/Amin/E7/Dmin/Amin/B^{b}7/E7/Amin/Dmin/E7/Amin/Bdim/E7/Amin

2. F/Gmin7-C7/F/Gmin7-C7/F/Gmin7-C7/F

3. F/F/G7/G7/Gmin7/C7/F/F

4. E^b-Fmin7/F7-E^b/F7-B^{b}7/E^b/A^b-E^b

g. Complete this sequential pattern until the starting chord is reached again:

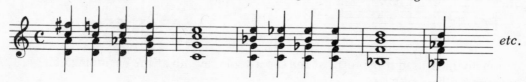

etc.

EXERCISE 7: Using the Super-Tonic Sevenths in Harmonizing Melodies

When harmonizing a melody:

1. Find beginnings and ends of phrases and decide on cadence chords.

2. Look at the melody to see possible chord outlines.

3. When there is a leap in the melody, the chances are that the tone left by leap is a chord tone.

4. Study the harmonic rhythm. If chords seem to change on the first and third beats at the beginning of a melody in triple meter, try to continue this rate of chord change—except at cadence points, where the harmonic rhythm often speeds up.

5. Work from the known to the unknown: find places where the harmony is obvious; then fill in the other chords.

6. When working out the scheme for a harmonization, keep the left-hand part as simple as possible. After the harmonic choices have been made, try different accompaniment styles to see which is most appropriate.

In each of the following melodies, there is at least one place where the super-tonic can be used:

a. In these melodies, the diatonic super-tonic triad or seventh moves to the V or V^7:

1. Mazas: Opus 36

2. "Du, du liegst mir im Herzen" (German)

3. Nursery tune

b. The super-tonic moves to a tonic $^6_4$ at least once in each of these melodies:

1. Haydn: *The Creation*

2. "Come, Thou Almighty King"

I_4^6

3. Mozart: *The Marriage of Figaro*

(P. T.)

(P.T. P.T.)

c. The II^7, functioning usually, but not always, as a V7 of V, can be substituted for the diatonic ii^7 or ii^{o7}. It is often used at semi-cadence points, as in No. 1 below, where the melody descends from scale degree 2 to 5, suggesting the key of G. In each of the following melodies there is at least one place where the II^7 can be used. Where there is a choice of ii^7 or II^7, the ear, as always, should be the ultimate guide.

1. American Fiddling Tune

G: 5———— 1

2. Mason: "Uxbridge"

A - men.

3. "Jungfräulein, soll ich mit dich geh'n?" (German)

Allegro

4. "All Through the Night" (Welsh)

Andante

5. Foster: "Beautiful Dreamer"

6. *St. Catherine Hymn*, "Faith of Our Fathers"

7. Schubert: "Die Forelle"

d. Composers sometimes use several forms of the super-tonic seventh, thereby achieving interesting chromatic effects, as in this ending of a song by Schumann:

Schumann: "An meinen Herzen"

Play the Schumann example above, filling in the harmonies that are not indicated. Then use the harmonic plan as the basis for several improvisations.

EXERCISE 8: Ear Training

Play by ear the following well-known melodies. Harmonize them, using diatonic or chromatic super-tonic triads or sevenths:

1. "Bendemeer's Stream"
2. "Flow Gently, Sweet Afton"
3. "The British Grenadiers"
4. "Love Somebody"
5. "Jesus Shall Reign Where'ere the Sun"
6. "Faith of Our Fathers"
7. "My Faith Looks up to Thee"
8. "Sally in Our Alley"
9. "Oh Dear, What Can the Matter Be"
10. "My Bonnie Lies Over the Ocean"
11. "Happy Birthday"
12. "Captain Jinks"
13. "The Ash Grove"
14. "Home on the Range"
15. "Londonderry Air"
16. "Here We Go Round the Mulberry Bush"
17. "Tramp, Tramp, Tramp"
18. "Oh, Dem Golden Slippers"
19. "In the Cross of Christ I Glory"
20. "Deck the Halls"

13
THE SUB-MEDIANT
HARMONIES

The **sub-mediant** chord is built on the sixth degree of the diatonic scale. It consists of the scale degrees 6-8(1)-3.

EXERCISE 1: Finding and Building the Sub-Mediant

a. Play the D major scale ascending, following it with the triad built on the sixth scale degree:

Note that in major, the sub-mediant triad is a *minor* triad (vi). Repeat the above exercise in the major keys of F, A^b, E, B^b, and C$^\sharp$.

b. In the harmonic minor, the sub-mediant triad is *major* (VI):

Repeat the above exercise in the harmonic minor keys of G, B, F$^\sharp$, C, and G$^\sharp$.

c. Build a minor triad on each of the given pitches; follow each triad with the major scale of which the triad is vi — remembering that the sixth degree of the major scale is a minor third below the tonic:

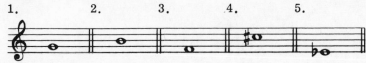

d. Build a major triad on each of the following pitches; follow each triad with the harmonic minor scale of which the triad is VI—remembering that the sixth degree of the harmonic minor scale is a major third below the tonic:

EXERCISE 2: The Uses of the Sub-Mediant

Since the normal progression of chords in traditional harmony is through the circle of fifths, the sub-mediant (vi) would move to the super-tonic (ii) as follows in the key of G major:

vi – ii – V – I

a. Think of each of these bass tones as being the root of a vi, and resolve them as in the examples above.

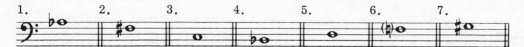

b. Repeat the chord progressions given at the beginning of this exercise (vi-ii-V-I) in the key of G harmonic minor. Then think of each of the following bass tones as the root of a VI, and resolve it through the ii°-V-i progression:

c. The progression of vi or VI through the circle of fifths occurs often at cadence points. Here are two examples which should be analyzed and then transposed to at least four other keys:

1. Bach: Chorale cadence

2. Mozart: *Don Giovanni*

d. The sub-mediant is also used in opening phrases, as well as in cadential phrases such as those given above. Popular songs such as "Blue Moon" have been based on the I-vi-ii-V^7 progression, as was the vaudeville "vamp till ready":

Transpose the I-vi-ii-V^7 progression illustrated above to at least four other keys. Then use it as a basis for improvisations, playing the progression three times and adding a two-measure I-V-I or I-IV-I cadence.

e. The sub-mediant harmony is often used as a replacement for the tonic: for the sake of variety, as in No. 1 below, or as a substitute for the tonic, as in Nos. 2 and 3 below, in order to delay a cadence. This technique creates what is known as a **deceptive cadence** (V-VI or V-vi).

1. Bach: Chorale, "Schmücke dich, o liebe Seele"

2. Mozart: *The Abduction from the Seraglio*

3. Mozart: Piano Sonata, K. 333

Analyze the examples above. Then transpose each one to at least four other keys.

f. Harmonize these short melodies. Look for places where the vi or VI can be used as a replacement for the tonic:

1. Corelli: Violin Sonata No. 6

2. Hymn tune, "Dundee"

3. Bizet: *Carmen*

4. Purcell: *King Arthur*

5. Chorale, "Ermuntre dich, mein schwacher Geist"

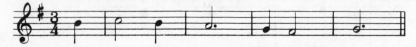

g. The vi is sometimes preceded by a V_6 when the melody is based on scale degrees 3-5-8:

Find at least one place to use the progression V_6-vi in the following melody:

"Billy Boy" (American)

h. In the following sequential pattern, the vi or VI of one key becomes a new tonic, alternating major and minor. Continue the pattern until the original G-major triad is reached again:

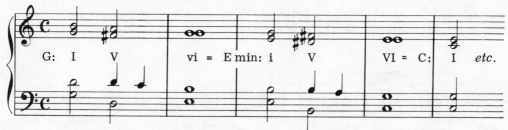

i. The sub-mediant, like its relative the tonic, is a comparatively free chord in its progressions. In earlier examples it was shown moving to the V and the ii. It can also move, in a sort of "circle of thirds," to the IV, as in this example from Wagner's *Parsifal:*

Play the following progressions in the major and minor forms of at least six keys. Start some of the progressions with the third or the fifth of the tonic in the soprano:

| maj.: | I | vi | IV | ii | I$^6_4$ | V | I | | I | vi | IV | ii7 | I$^6_4$ | V7 | I |
| min.: | i | VI | iv | ii° | i$^6_4$ | V | i | | i | VI | iv | ii°7 | i$^6_4$ | V7 | i |

Improvise short pieces based on the harmonic pattern given above. Start by singing melodies over accompaniment patterns such as this one:

Improvise études, waltzes, etc. based on the above patterns. Stretch each harmony over two measures, and introduce a passing tone in the bass that converts each triad into a seventh chord in alternate measures, as in this beginning:

i   i$^4_2$ VI

j. The sub-mediant sometimes moves back to a tonic, making a rather calm, static progression, as in the opening of Wagner's *Lohengrin*:

Wagner: *Lohengrin*

Adagio

Experiment using a vi moving to a I as in this folk-like style:

k. The sub-mediant usually occurs as a triad in root position. It is, however, sometimes used in first inversion, as in this harmonization by Bach:

Bach: Chorale, "Nun danket alle Gott"

Analyze the example above, and transpose it to four other keys.

EXERCISE 3: The Sub-Mediant Seventh and the Altered Sub-Mediant

The sub-mediant can be enriched by the addition of sevenths and ninths.

a. The vi^7 is often used in harmonizing scale degrees 5-4-3-2. Analyze this chorale harmonization and transpose it to four other keys:

Bach: Chorale, "O Ewigkeit, du Donnerwort"

b. The most common chromatic change applied to the sub-mediant is the conversion of the vi to a VI by raising the third of the chord, making it, in effect, the dominant of the super-tonic:

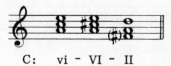

C: vi - VI - II

Practice playing these progressions, in which the vi and the ii have been made into dominant sevenths. Transpose to at least four major keys:

I vi ii6 V7   I   I VI7 II7 V7   I   I VI7 II9 V7   I

c. The VI$_4^6$ is sometimes used between the two positions of the super-tonic, as well as appearing in its more usual root position. Note how Schumann, in the example below, manages to extend his harmonic phrase. Transpose the example to three other keys:

Schumann: *Novelette in F*

col 8va IV V$_3^4$ I6   VI   ii6   VI$_4^6$ ii

d. Analyze this progression and transpose it to the keys of E^b, A, C$^\sharp$, B^b, and F. Note the harmonization of the melodic progression 2-3-4-5, and its reverse, (5)-4-3-2:

e. Use the VI$_4^6$ in the final phrases of the verse and chorus of this hymn:

"Shall We Gather at the River?"

Con moto

2   3   4

V7

2   3   4

ii6   VI$_4^6$ ii V7

f. Fill in the harmonies of "America," noting the $\sharp\text{v}^\circ 7^\circ$, a diminished seventh chord made by raising the root of the dominant, which moves to vi in measure 4. Transpose this harmonization to five other major keys:

g. Review some of the melodies given earlier in this chapter, and experiment by changing some of the V^7's to $\sharp\text{v}^\circ 7^\circ$'s.

h. In some styles of popular music, the VI^7 slips down a half step to the $^\flat\text{VI}^7$, instead of resolving to a ii. The $^\flat\text{VI}^7$, in turn, might slip down to a V^7. Analyze the example below; then transpose it to four other keys. Note that the VI, the $^\flat\text{VI}$, and the V all have ninths added above their sevenths:

i. The given figured basses are first to be realized in four-part harmony, and then to be improvised on melodically:

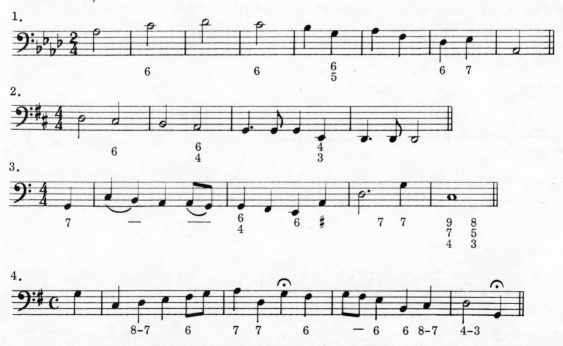

5.

6.

j. Improvise melodic lines based on these guitar-chord indications:

1. Em7/A7/Bm/Bm/Em7/A7/Bm/Bm/Em7/A7/Bm/Bm/G/A7/D

2. Gm/D7/E^b/Cm7/D/D7/Gm/Gm7/C7/D7/E^b/Cm/D7/Gm

EXERCISE 4: Harmonizing Melodies with the Sub-Mediant

Harmonize the following melodies, each of which has in it at least one opportunity to use some form of the sub-mediant. Look for places where the vi or VI will add variety, delay a cadence, replace a tonic in an harmonic progression, or be useful as a V or V^7 of the super-tonic. As in previous harmonizations of melodies, first block out phrases, select the cadences, and be aware of harmonic rhythm. In a few cases, an accompaniment style or rhythmic figure is suggested, or a few key chords are indicated. After choosing the harmonies, various accompaniment patterns might be tried. Do not make everything sound like four-part vocal writing; *the harmonizations should be for the piano.*

1. "The Minstrel Boy" (Irish)

2. "Cockles and Mussels" (Irish)

3. "Ho Jeanette" (French)

4. "Crusader's Hymn" (German)

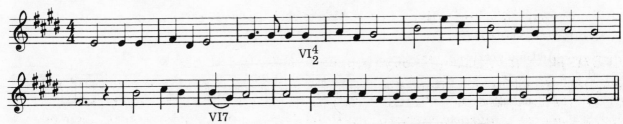

5. Mason: "When I Behold the Wondrous Cross"

6. Chorale, "Es stehn vor Gottes Throne"

7. Schubert: "Frühlingssehnsucht"

Vivace

8. Chorale, "Aus meines Herzens Grunde"

I♭7   IV

9. Mendelssohn: *Songs Without Words*

#v°7°

10. Mozart: Piano Sonata, K. 331

Andante grazioso

11. Purcell: *King Arthur*

vi7   II7   IV7

12. Giordani: "Caro mio ben"

13. Schubert: "Mein" *(note melodic sequences, to be matched harmonically)*

14

THE MEDIANT HARMONIES
Phrygian Cadences

The **mediant** harmony, built on the third degree of the scale, is so different in its major and minor scale forms that it will be treated in two sections.

EXERCISE 1: The Mediant Harmony in Major

The triad built on the third scale degree includes scale tones 3-5-7, and is a minor triad (iii):

a. Play the first two tones of a major scale, followed by the mediant triad of that scale in its various positions:

Each of the following two-note figures represents the first and second degrees of a major scale. Follow each group with the iii of the key, as above:

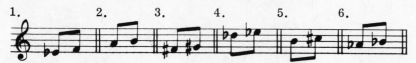

b. Continue this sequential pattern in which I moves to its iii until the first chord is reached again:

c. As with previously presented diatonic chords, the iii progresses normally to the chord whose root lies a fifth lower, in this case the vi. Here is the diatonic circle of fifths in the key of C, starting on three different positions of I:

1. Play the exercise above in the keys of B^b, D, A^b, $F^\sharp$, D^b, and B.

2. Improvise études, dances, and lyrical pieces based on the harmonic progression I-iii-vi-ii-V^7-I. Experiment in lengthening the improvisations by letting the flow of the music determine the duration of each chord and by repeating the harmonic pattern.

d. The mediant can resolve to the dominant, and from there to the tonic. The example below shows a iii in C major followed by the V_4^3 and I of that key:

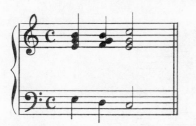

Consider each of these bass tones to be the root of a mediant triad. Move each iii to the V_4^3-I of the correct key, as in the example above:

EXERCISE 2: Uses of the Mediant

Like the sub-mediant, the mediant has two tones in common with the tonic chord. It also has two tones in common with the dominant chord. Possibly, because the mediant chord contains the seventh scale degree, it is more closely related to the dominant harmony than to the tonic:

Just as the vi is sometimes used as a replacement for I, so the iii is used to replace the V.

a. The iii is often used to harmonize the seventh scale degree in a descending scale line 8-7-6-(5). Analyze the following example and transpose it to the keys of F, D, B, and G^b:

Bach: Chorale, "Nun lob', mein Seel', den Herren"

I   vi   iii   IV   V$\frac{4}{2}$ I6   ii$\frac{6}{5}$ V   I

b. The mediant chord in first inversion often occurs as a replacement for the V or the I$\frac{6}{4}$. Analyze the examples below, and transpose them to at least four other major keys. (The iii in the first example could be considered a dominant with a suspension held over from the tonic, or it might be designated a dominant thirteenth.)

Monk: "Abide with Me"

iii6   V7

iii6

c. The following sequential patterns use the iii$_6$ moving to V. Carry out each pattern until the starting chord is reached again. In the first pattern, after the C-major triad is reached, start the pattern again on B^b and A:

1. (a)   (b)   (c)

2.

d. The vi-iii$_6$ progression often occurs as a parallel progression to I-V$_6$, as in Beethoven's Piano Sonata, Opus 79:

The outer voices of the Beethoven example make a melodic two-part counterpoint:

Make at least four variations on the Beethoven harmonic/melodic pattern. Change the meter, as shown in this possible variation:

(Pianists might play the opening phrases of Chopin's "Butterfly" Étude, and the Gavotte from Bach's *French Suite* No. 5, comparing them with the Beethoven example given above.)

EXERCISE 3: Phrygian Cadences

As with the super-tonic and the sub-mediant, chromatic alterations can be made in the mediant chord. The most common chromatic change is to raise the third of the chord in a major key, transforming the minor iii to a major chord. This major III is often the resolution of a **Phrygian cadence**, so-called because the movement of the outer voices suggests a cadence in the Phrygian mode:

a. Play Phrygian cadences in the keys of F, A, E^b, and B.

b. The Phrygian cadence is a basic ingredient of Spanish Gypsy music. Improvise florid melodic lines over the ii$_6$-III progression:

c. The Phrygian cadence is especially useful when scale degrees 1-2-3 are repeated in a melody, as in the folk tune "Annie Laurie":

Transpose the above to the keys of B^b, G, F, and D.

EXERCISE 4: Using the III and the III^7

The possibilities of the mediant chord in major are further expanded when sevenths or ninths are added to the chromatically altered chord: the major III in major.

a. The III or III^7 is often used as the V or V^7 of vi:

Transpose this phrase to the keys of A^b, C, F, and E^b.

b. In the following pattern, the V$_6$-I progression is paralleled by III$_6$-vi and II$_6$-V. Analyze the melodic-harmonic plan of this example, and play it in the keys of E^b, B, F$^\sharp$, A^b, and D^b:

c. Possibly the best-known use of the III⁷ is at the beginning of Liszt's *Liebestraum.* Here the III⁷ progresses through the circle of fifths to the I, but with each chord made into a V⁷ or V⁹:

Play the Liszt harmonic pattern in block chords. Transpose the progression to the keys of E, C, G♭, and C♯. Then improvise short pieces based on the pattern.

d. Harmonize these melodies in a free pianistic style. Each melody has at least one place where a form of the mediant can be used:

4. Croft: "Oh God Our Help in Ages Past"

5. Lawes: "Gather Ye Rosebuds"

6. Schubert: "Mit dem grünen Lautenbande"

ii6 III   V$\frac{4}{2}$

7. Balfe: "The Bohemian Girl"

Andante

e. The following figured basses include forms of the mediant. Realize the basses, first in four-part harmony, and then with interesting melodies:

1.

f. Improvise on the following guitar-chord patterns which include forms of the mediant:

1. C-Em/Dm7-G7/C-Em/Dm7-G7/C-Em/Dm7-G7/E7/A7/D7/G7/C-F7/C

2. F/Gm7-C7/F/Am-C7/F/Am7-F/Gm7/A7/Dm7/G7/C/D7/Gm/Gm7-C7/F

3. A-F♯m/D-E7/A/D/A/F♯m-C♯m/Bm-F♯7-Bm-B7/E9/A-C♯m/D-A/E7/A

EXERCISE 5: The Mediant in Minor

There are two forms of the mediant harmony in minor. In the harmonic minor scale, the mediant triad is augmented (III+):

III+

In the natural minor, the mediant chord is a major triad (III):

III

The example below shows the first two tones of a minor scale followed by the two forms of the mediant to be found in minor:

III+   III

a. Consider each of the given two-tone groups as first and second scale degrees in minor. Play them, following each group with the two forms of the mediant of the scales they indicate, as above:

b. The III+ often sounds as though the V were being decorated, as in this example by Stradella, which uses the III+ to harmonize the third scale degree. This, in turn, moves down to the second scale degree, making a V triad:

Stradella: "Ombre, voi che celate"

V   III⁺₆   V   VI   i6   —   i⁶₄   V   i

La Flora, Vol. I, Wilhelm Hansen, Copenhagen, 1949. Used by permission of G. Schirmer, Inc., sole selling agents.

Transpose the Stradella example to at least three other minor keys. Then analyze the two examples below, and transpose them to three other keys:

1. Bach: Partita in B Minor

2. Chopin: Mazurka, Opus 50

c. The III+ is often found in first inversion, as in the examples given above. When this occurs, the bass tone (the third of the chord) is usually doubled. The examples given below show the use of the III+₆ in harmonizing various scale degrees. Analyze the examples and transpose them to the keys of B, D, G, C, and E minor:

A min.: III⁺₆ VI

d. Harmonize the following melodic fragments, using the III+ at least once in each harmonization:

e. The III in minor is frequently found in music of the Baroque period. This music often shifts back and forth from the minor key to its relative major. *The III chord of the minor key is the tonic chord of the relative major.* It is sometimes preceded by its own dominant:

Analyze and continue the following sequential pattern until the starting chord is reached again. Repeat the pattern starting in C minor and then B^b minor:

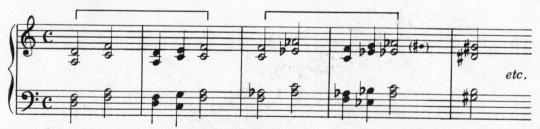

f. Analyze the following chorale harmonization and transpose it to the keys of G, F, E, B, and C:

Bach: Chorale, "Ach wie nichtig, ach wie flüchtig"

g. The III or III^7 can be used to harmonize the lowered seventh degree of the scale:

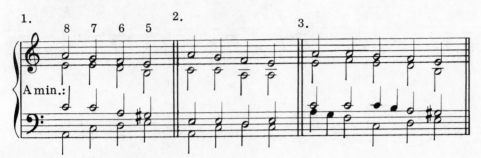

h. It can be used to give harmonic variety to a chord progression, and to act as a substitute for the tonic:

i. Analyze the preceding progressions and harmonizations of scale segments. Transpose each example to at least four other minor keys. Then improvise on the harmonic patterns, stretching out the time given to each chord.

j. Harmonize the following melodic fragments, using the III at least once in each harmonization:

k. Harmonize the following unfigured basses. In each example there is an opportunity to use the III at least once. In some instances, the III may be preceded by its own V:

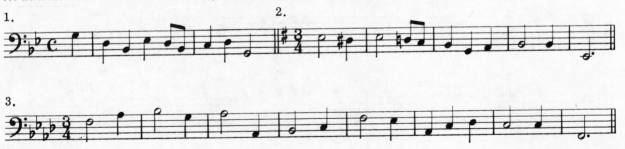

EXERCISE 6: Harmonizing Melodies with Mediant Chords

a. The following melodies are to be harmonized using iii, iii^7, III^7, III+, and III. As in previous chapters, first block out the harmony; then find an appropriate style of accompaniment for the melody. In some cases, see if a single bass note will be sufficient to suggest a harmony. In other cases, the accompaniment might be florid:

1. Edson: "Awake My Soul, Arise"

2. Cornell: "Let Zion's Watchmen All Awake"

III7 IV

3. Reinagle: "Come O Thou All-Victorious Lord"

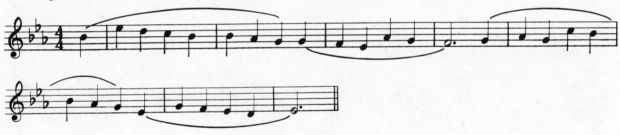

4. Neumark: "Leave God To Order All Thy Ways"

5. Chorale, "Wer weiss, wie nahe mir mein Ende"

6. Chorale, "Valet will ich dir geben"

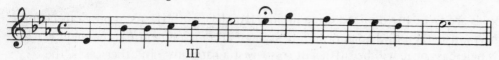

III

7. Chorale, "Nun lob', mein Seel', den Herren"

8. Chorale, "In Dulci Jubilo"

III

9. Chorale, "Verleih' uns Frieden gnädiglich"

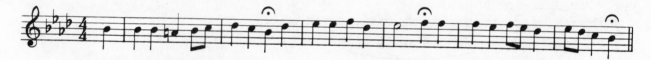

10. "Once I Loved a Maiden Fair" (English)

Andantino

iii   I♭7   ii6   III

11. "Paper of Pins" (American)

12. "Who Will Shoe Your Pretty Little Foot" (American)

Andante

13. Franz: "Frühlingsgedrange"

Allegretto

III7

14. Schubert: "Frühlingsglaube"

Andante sostenuto

III$\frac{4}{3}$

IV 6

b. Play the following chord patterns, first as block harmonies, then continuing the musical ideas of the first measure. (It is not necessary to have every measure exactly like the first one; use contrast when variety seems called for.)

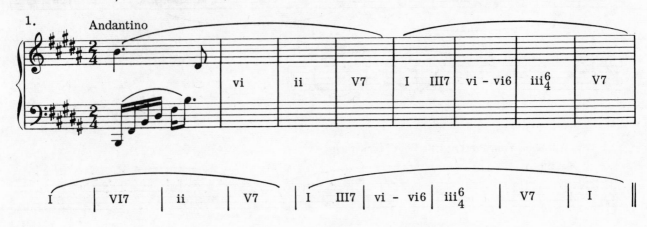

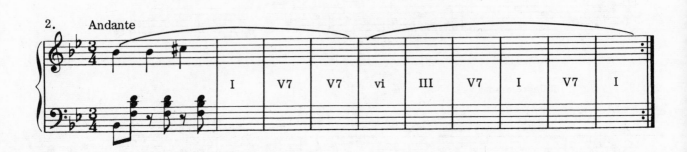

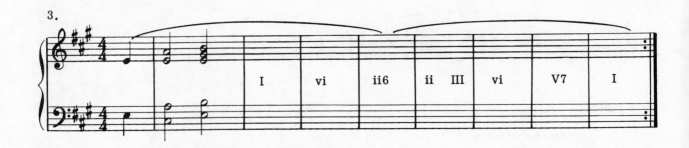

EXERCISE 7: Figured-Bass Realizations Using the Mediant

Realize the given figured basses. The first should be song-like, with an accompaniment in eighth notes, as indicated. Nos. 1 and 2 should be played first as four-voice chorales, then freely in pianistic style:

15

THE SUB-TONIC CHORDS
AND THE MINOR DOMINANT

EXERCISE 1: The Sub-Tonic Triad in Major and Harmonic Minor

The diatonic triad based on the sub-tonic or seventh scale degree of both the major and the harmonic minor scales is diminished:

a. Continue the following sequence through the circle of fifths until the starting tone has been reached again:

b. In the following exercise the given tone is the tonic. Resolve the sub-tonic, or vii° of that key to the major and minor tonics, as shown in the first example:

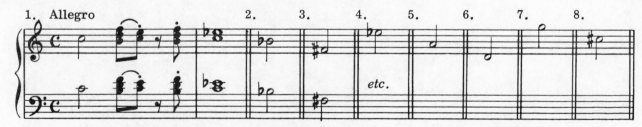

c. The given tones represent the roots of vii° chords. Play the triad and resolve it, first to the major tonic, then to the minor tonic, as in the first example:

EXERCISE 2: Uses of the vii°

a. The vii° in root position is found most often in sequential patterns following the circle of fifths. Play and analyze the following progression. Then transpose it to the keys of B♭, D, A♭, F♯, and E♭:

b. Repeat the above pattern using these chord positions:

c. Improvise short motives that can be used in sequence over the preceding harmonic patterns, as in this example:

(The circle of fifths involving the vii° is found principally in the major mode and in the harmonic minor. Discussion of the ♭VII in the natural minor comes later in this chapter.)

d. The vii° occurs most often in first inversion, with the bass tone—the third of the chord—doubled. In most cases, the vii°$_6$ functions as a member of the V^7 family, and is used between the root position and the first inversion of the tonic:

1. Brahms: Sonata for Violin and Piano, Opus 100

2. Purcell: Bonduca

Play and analyze the examples above and transpose each one to at least four other keys.

e. The vii°$_6$ is useful in harmonizing the following scale-degree patterns: 1-2-3; 3-2-1; 3-4-5; 5-4-3; 6-7-8; 8-7-8. Note the resolutions of the interval of the augmented fourth in going from vii°$_6$ to the tonic. Transpose each of the following examples to at least five other keys. Then invent pianistic figures that follow the same melodic/harmonic plans:

f. Scale degrees 6-7-8 in minor require the use of the melodic minor rather than the harmonic form:

g. The vii°₆ often appears between a super-tonic and a tonic, especially in Bach's chorale harmonizations. Analyze and transpose the following:

Bach: Chorale, "Mach's mit mir, Gott, nach deiner Güt"

The ii-vii°₆ progression is especially helpful in harmonizing scale degrees 4-3 or 4-5:

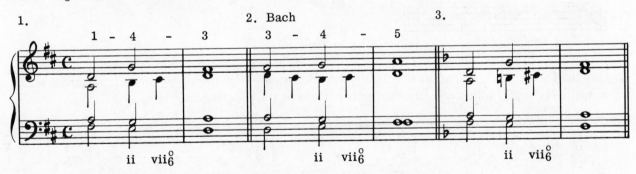

Harmonize the following short melodies using the ii-vii°₆ progression:

h. Harmonize the following short melodies, each of which has at least one place to use a vii° or a vii°6:

i. Realize the following figured basses, each of which includes at least one vii° or vii°6:

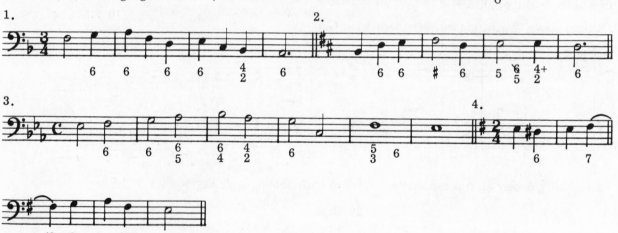

j. Play the following chord patterns in the rhythm indicated. Then improvise on each pattern in a pianistic style, still adhering to the rhythmic pattern of the progression:

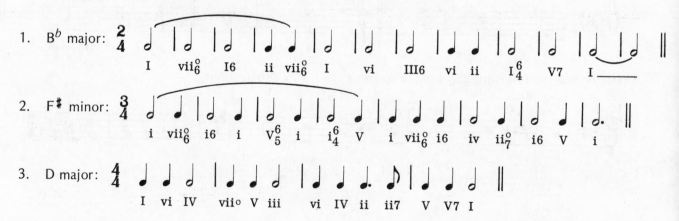

EXERCISE 3: The Major Sub-Tonic Triad (bVII)

In the natural minor scale the sub-tonic chord is a major triad (*b*VII):

a. Practice playing *b*VII's in the scales of the given keynotes, following the pattern given in No. 1 below:

b. One of the most common uses of the *b*VII is as the dominant of the mediant in minor. Play and analyze each of the musical examples below. Transpose each example to at least four other keys:

1. Mendelssohn: **Songs without Words**

2. Mattheson: **Sarabande**

3. Chopin: **Mazurka, Opus 67, No. 2**

4. Bach: Chorale, "Erhalt'uns, Herr, bei deinem Wort"

c. Play and analyze the following example. Then use the harmonic pattern as a basis for a set of variations:

Handel: Sonata for Flute

d. The following progression is a common one in certain types of Spanish music:

Granados: *Goyescas*

Improvise pieces based on the harmonic pattern of the Granados above, playing the pattern two or three times before adding a cadential phrase that ends on the tonic chord.

e. The ^{b}VII is often used by composers in a diatonic circle of fifths, as in Handel's Passacaglia in G minor, quoted below. (The passacaglia is usually in a triple meter; Handel's work is an exception to the rule.) Play and analyze the example. Then transpose the progression to the minor keys of F, B, E^b, and F$^\sharp$, improvising at least two variations in each key. Feel free to change the meter:

f. Harmonize the following melodies, each of which has at least one place to use a ^{b}VII or ^{b}VII$_6$:

1. Chorale, "Gieb dich zufrieden"

2. "Ay! Linda Amiga" (Spanish)

3.

g. Realize the following figured basses, each of which includes a ^{b}VII or ^{b}VII$_6$:

1.

2.

EXERCISE 4: The Minor Dominant

The minor dominant triad (v) is diatonic in the natural minor scale. It is related to the ^{b}VII in that in both chords the seventh scale degree lies a whole step below the tonic:

a. Practice playing v₆'s in the natural minor scales of the given keynotes, in the manner of No. 1 below:

b. The v₆ is often used when the composer desires a smooth, step-wise bass:

Purcell: Minuet

Transpose the Purcell phrase above to the minor keys of F♯, D, B♭, and E♭.

c. The v is useful in harmonizing modal music. Tchaikovsky, in this harmonization of a Russian folk melody, uses the v as well as the ♭VII. Play and analyze the example, and transpose it to at least three other keys:

Tchaikovsky (arr.): "Russian Folk Song"

d. Harmonize these folk melodies, using minor dominants to maintain a modal quality:

1. "The Turtle Dove" (English)

2. Russian folk tune

Allegro moderato

3. Russian

e. An important Baroque form was a series of variations built on a ground bass, a repeated short pattern four or eight measures in length. One of the favorite ground basses was a four-note figure that descended step-wise from the tonic to the dominant in minor:

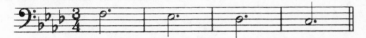

The lowered seventh degree gave the composer freedom to use a ^{b}VII or a v. In his F-minor Chaconne, Pachelbel harmonizes the bass pattern in several ways:

Experiment with the four-note ground bass. See how many harmonizations you can discover. Introduce other tones between the principal tones, giving opportunities for additional harmonies. Build variations.

f. Harmonize the melodies and realize the basses given below. In each case, a v or v₆ is used at least once:

EXERCISE 5: The Diminished Seventh Chord

The seventh chord built on the seventh scale degree in the harmonic minor is a **diminished seventh chord** (vii°7°):

While the vii°7° is a chord derived from the minor scale, it is equally at home in the major keys.

a. Practice playing vii°7°'s in the scales of the given keynotes, in the manner of No. 1 below:

b. The given notes below represent the roots of vii°7° chords. Resolve each to its proper tonic, as in No. 1:

c. Continue the following sequences until the beginning chord is reached again:

d. Play and analyze the following pattern which uses the vii°7° in all positions, noting the resolutions of the tones of the vii°7°. Transpose the pattern to the harmonic minor keys of B, G, D, F♯, and E♭:

e. This sequence goes through a circle of fourths. Continue it until the starting chord is reached again. Note that the third of each tonic becomes the top tone of the new vii°7°:

EXERCISE 6: Uses of the Diminished Seventh Chord

The vii°7° can be used in any of its positions to harmonize scale tones 7-2-4-6, usually in place of a dominant. Brahms, along with Bach and Mozart, used the vii°7° in masterful fashion. In his Waltz No. 9, he harmonized the seventh scale degree with two different positions of the vii°7°, thus achieving a melodic bass. In the next to last measure of the excerpt quoted below, an embellishing vii°7° to the iv is used:

a. Make several improvisations based on the harmonic pattern of the Brahms Waltz, adding cadences when logical.

b. Harmonize the following melodies, each of which has at least one place where a vii°7° may be used:

1. Schubert: "Eifersucht und Stolz"

2. Schubert: "Der Greise Kopf"

Poco lento

16

MISCELLANEOUS ITEMS
CONCERNING DIATONIC HARMONY
Diatonic Seventh Chords; Achieving Contrapuntal
Motion over an Harmonic Pattern; Harmonic Variations;
The Chaconne and Passacaglia; Melodic Variations

DIATONIC SEVENTH CHORDS

The addition of sevenths, or even ninths, to diatonic triads adds harmonic variety to music while changing the function or progression of the chords very little. The one general principle to remember when dealing with seventh chords is that the seventh usually resolves downward. The following exercises provide some experience in dealing with seventh chords, both in harmonizing melodies and in improvising.

EXERCISE 1: Experimenting with Diatonic Seventh Chords

a. Play, analyze, and then transpose the following pattern to the keys of B^b, D, A^b, E, and D^b:

b. In minor, care should be taken when dealing with the seventh scale degree. Generally, in sequential patterns, the natural minor form is used, especially in descending lines, *except when the seventh scale degree returns to the tonic*. Play, analyze, and then transpose the following patterns to the minor keys of D, G, B^b, A, and E:

1.

254

2.

c. Complete the following decorated sequential patterns which are based on the progressions given in the exercises above. Then transpose them to the keys of G, B, E, D, and F♯:

5.

6.

d. Most sequences involving seventh chords move downward, because of the resolutions of the
    sevenths of the chords. Play and analyze this *ascending* pattern; then transpose it to the major
    keys of A, E^b, B, G^b, and D. Then play the original pattern in C *minor*, making whatever adjust-
    ments are necessary. Play the pattern in the minor keys of G, F, B, and E:

e. Some series of seventh chords are derived from a chain of suspensions, as in the following pro-
    gression. Play it, analyze it, and transpose it to the major and minor keys of D, F, G, B^b, and A.
    As in previous progressions, the natural form of the minor scale is used except for the final
    cadence:

f. By using secondary dominants, such as the II^7 resolving to the V, and by using embellishing
    diminished sevenths, a great deal of variety can be achieved in harmonizing a descending scale:

Analyze the following examples of scale harmonization, and play them in four other keys. The examples show mixtures of triads and sevenths. Scale tones are repeated—but not returned to:

g. Invent other ways of harmonizing ascending and descending scales.

h. Seventh chords mixed with triads can be used to add spice to the harmonization of melodies. The examples below show how a simple nursery tune could be harmonized in the most obvious way (No. 1), and then a bit more unexpectedly (No. 2):

"Mistress Mary"

Experiment with the harmonization of simple folk tunes, using combinations of triads and seventh chords.

i. Invent harmonic phrases using seventh chords and improvise on them. Here are several, taken from musical works, that use diatonic and chromatic sevenths:

1. E major: 4/4 vi $|$ii^7 $|$ V^7 $|$ I^7 $|$ IV^7 $|$ VII^7 $|$ III $\frown$ III $|$ iii^7 $|$ vi^7 $|$ II^7 $|$ V^7 $|$ I^7 $|$ IV^7 ii^7 $|$ V^7 $|$ I $\frown$ I $\|$

2. A^b major: 4/4 I $|$ vi^7 $|$ ii^7 $|$ V^7 $|$ I^7 $|$ VI^7 $|$ ii^7 $|$ I^{b7} $\frown$ I^{b7} $|$ IV^7 - ii^7 $|$ vii^{o7} - V^7 $|$ I $\frown$ I $\|$

3. D major: Lento 2/4 I - V^7 $|$ V^7 - I^7 $|$ I^{b7} - IV^7 $|$ III^7 - vi $|$ II^7 - V $|$ I - I^7 $|$ V - vi^7 $|$ iii - IV^7 $|$ I $\frown$ I $\|$

ACHIEVING CONTRAPUNTAL MOTION OVER AN HARMONIC PATTERN

The ability to improvise in simple contrapuntal styles is one that requires a certain amount of skill. It is also one that depends upon the understanding of a few basic principles. Bach, in his Chorale-Prelude, "Alle Menschen müssen sterben," harmonizes the chorale tune in a conventional way:

I   vi II7 V - 7 I6   IV   vii - V7 I   *etc.*

By the introduction of a little rhythmic figure using neighboring tones, Bach adds interest to the tune:

etc.

Even a plain i-V-i progression takes on added interest when it is treated in this fashion:

Walther: "Christ Who Makes Us Blessed"

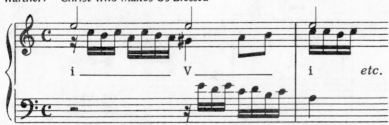

i _____ V _____   i   *etc.*

EXERCISE 2: Improvising Contrapuntal Patterns from an Harmonic Outline

The following examples should be tried in at least four other major or minor keys:

a. Take a basic harmonic progression such as:

Move one voice at a time, first in quarter notes, then with more rhythmic activity. Use passing tones and neighboring tones:

Using an elaborated melody, add another voice in parallel thirds or parallel sixths:

The i-V-i pattern can be transformed, as in the following examples. Duets can be made between various pairs of voices, using parallel thirds. After transposing the examples, invent other ways of using parallel thirds or sixths over the i-V-i pattern:

Adding "escape" tones (échappées), non-harmonic tones left by leap, gives another kind of melodic interest:

The interval of a third can be played against itself (in contrary motion):

as in this version of the i-V-i progression:

Melodic lines in contrary motion can be made to converge on the desired interval:

A line in one voice can be imitated in another voice:

Experiment to see how many contrapuntal ideas can be made to work over the i-V-i pattern.

b. Play the following sequential patterns based on parallel thirds and sixths until the first chord is reached again:

c. A series of thirds can be played in contrary motion, simply, as in No. 1 below, or filled in, as in No. 2. Complete the patterns below and invent other possibilities, using only thirds on the beat:

d. Thirds and sixths can alternate. Continue these sequential patterns until the starting tones are reached again:

e. Improvise contrapuntal motion over these harmonic phrases:

1.   D major: 2/4 I $|$ vi $|$ ii$_4^2$ V$_6$ $|$ vi ii $|$ V^7 I $|$ vi II^7 $|$ V V^7 $|$ I vi $|$ ii V^7 $|$ I $\|$

2.   E minor: 3/8 i $|$ ^{b}VII $|$ ^{b}VI $|$ III $|$ ii $|$ V^7 $|$ vii°$^{7°}$ $|$ i $\|$

3.   F minor: 3/4 i $|$ V i$_6$ $|$ iv V $|$ iv$_6$ iv $|$ V V$_3^4$ $|$ i$_6$ vii°$^{7°}$ $|$ i $\|$

4.   A major: 3/4 I $|$ V$_6$ $|$ V^7 $|$ I$_6$ $|$ vi^7 $|$ ii^7 $|$ V^7 $|$ I $|$ II^7 $|$ V $|$ V^7 $|$ I $\|$

f. Extract harmonic phrases from musical literature and use them as bases for contrapuntal improvisation. Use as much imitation as possible.

g. Harmonize the following chorale melodies and basses, using as much contrapuntal motion as you can. The chorale melody itself may be decorated. Harmonize in two, three, or four voices as seems practical. The last two melodies should be considered as middle-voice lines, with soprano and bass to be added around them:

HARMONIC VARIATIONS: THE CHACONNE AND PASSACAGLIA

An important Baroque variation form was the **chaconne**, as was its close relative, the **passacaglia**. Both were slow, stately dances in triple meter. The differences between these two forms can be described as uncertain; composers have used these names interchangeably. For our study of some of the techniques useful in making melodic and stylistic variations over a traditional chord pattern, we will designate the form as a chaconne.

The chaconne is built on a four- or eight-measure repeated harmonic phrase: the harmony here becomes the theme. To underline the solemnity of the dance, the harmonies change slowly: often there is only one chord to a bar. It was perhaps because the dance lasted for a long time, while its musical theme was essentially a short one, that musicians began the practice of making variations on the harmonic phrase, thus extending the music through variety rather than through simple repetition.

While the chaconne as a variation form developed during the Baroque period, it, like many musical forms, has persisted in one way or another up to the present. The concept of starting with a harmonic plan and making variations on it is the basis, for instance, for most jazz improvisations. The improvising group decides on a key and an harmonic plan (that of the "blues" has been the most popular) and invents musical ideas that fit the harmonic plan.

EXERCISE 3: Improvising Chaconne Variations

a. To make a chaconne theme, devise an harmonic plan consisting of two four-measure phrases, ending on the tonic. Use one chord per measure, except possibly at the cadence where a more rapid change of harmony might prove desirable. In choosing the harmonic plan, work for a strong, recognizable bass line, using inversions as well as root positions of the chords. For illustrative purposes, the opening measures might be I-V$_6$.

b. In a 3/4 meter, play the chords of your harmonic plan in the left hand, making each chord a dotted half note. For each measure, choose one melody tone that belongs to the harmony of the measure, and play it also as a dotted half note:

Make the melodic line as smooth as possible, trying to create some thirds or sixths between the bass and the soprano. It is a good idea to write out this eight-measure theme, both harmony and melody, and keep it in front of you as you improvise variations.

c. Use the rhythmic pattern of  in the right hand, except at the cadence. As much as possible, let the melody move by step; leaps should be made only from chord tones:

d. Use three quarter notes per measure, seeing how many melodic routes can be found between the chord tones on the first beats of the measures:

e. Play the chord with the right hand, moving the bass in quarter notes:

(Do not worry too much about doublings or parallel fifths and octaves at this point; it is more important to think about melodic and rhythmic motion. Refinement can come with practice.)

f. Make the melodic pattern a series of running eighth notes, except for the cadence measure. Again, aim at making as smooth a line as possible, keeping skips to a minimum:

g. Make melodies consisting only of chord tones:

h. Analyze the following examples, and try to carry out the musical ideas with your own chaconne theme. The examples show only a few possibilities. More may be found in chaconnes and ground basses by Purcell, Handel, and Pachelbel. (The chaconnes by French Baroque composers are not variations, but rondo forms.)

i. For the sake of variety, move to a different mode for several variations; if the theme is in major, move to the tonic (parallel) minor; if the theme is in minor, move to the tonic (parallel) or relative major:

j. Throughout the chaconne, aim at contrast; alternate activity so that each hand has interesting things to do. Move from variations with many running notes to ones with full chords, etc. Save the most exciting variations for the last.

k. Those who are interested might try improvising chaconnes using seventh and ninth chords or polychords such as:

MELODIC VARIATIONS

A theme for variations can be a melody rather than a harmony. The most successful melodic themes are ones with character and substance. Some of the features of the purely harmonic variations, as in the chaconne and passacaglia, can be found in variations that have a melody as their basis.

EXERCISE 4: Improvising Variations on a Melody

a. Try improvising variations on well-known tunes, using some of the chaconne and passacaglia techniques suggested above.

b. Try improvising variations on the melody itself. You can use the basic melody tones in slow motion, inserting new tones between them for decoration or connection. You can try extracting small groups of melody tones as motives, repeating them in a fast rhythm and devising new rhythms for them. You can shift a major melody into minor, or a minor one into major. Try shifting the entire melody into a new meter.

c. With a melody as a theme, there is the possibility of creating variations by using different harmonizations. Harmonize a simple, well-known tune in three different ways.

d. Although the melody is the basic theme, it is possible to extract the original harmonization of the theme, and make a variation on it.

e. Try extracting a characteristic rhythmic motif from the theme and using it as the basis for a variation on the melody or the harmony.

The number of variation forms available for study is very large. For a start, look at the keyboard variations of Handel, Mozart, and Beethoven, and the violin variations of Paganini. Analyze the themes and the way the composers have varied those themes. You will notice that in some cases the theme is used primarily as a framework on which to display virtuoso instrumental technique. For more complicated and more sophisticated variation techniques, look at Brahms' *Variations on a Theme of Handel* for solo piano, and the variations both Brahms and Rachmaninoff have written on a theme of Paganini.

17
MODULATION

Modulation is the act and process of moving from one key center to another. Key changes can be gradual, as in No. 1 below, or abrupt, as in No. 2:

1. Bach: Invention

2. Scarlatti: Sonata, L. S. 2 (K. 420)

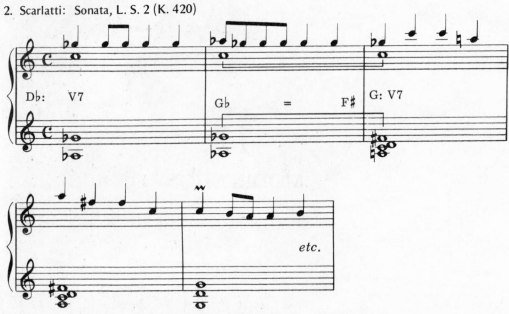

Edited by R. Kirkpatrick. Used by permission of G. Schirmer, Inc., sole selling agents.

In the Bach *Invention*, the composer moves the listener gradually from one tonality (D minor) to another (F major). There is even a brief moment, in measures 3 and 4, when the listener is not sure where he is tonally. In the Scarlatti, the change of key is immediate, and the effect is surprising. The process used by Bach is that of modulation by means of common or pivot chords. The function of Bach's modulation is structural: to move from one key to another, weakening the first key while preparing the listener for the new one. Here previous material may be repeated, with the freshness of a new tonality, or new material may be introduced with the new tonality. The process used by Scarlatti is called modulation by common or pivot tones. Its function is coloristic rather than structural.

EXERCISE 1: Modulation by Means of a Common Chord

Play the Bach *Invention* above in block harmony. Note that in measures 3 and 4 two chords are used that are each common to the keys of D minor and F major:

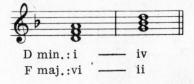

D min.: i —— iv
F maj.: vi ' —— ii

> *Bach could have turned back from either chord and remained in D minor. Instead, he moved on through a circle of fifths toward F major. Viewing a chord in this way, as being common to two keys, is the basic principle of common-chord modulation. Put it another way: modulation by common chord is like walking down a street until an intersection is reached. At the point where the two streets cross (the intersection: the common chord), one can continue on the same street, or turn off onto the other street.*

a. Reviewing the types of chords to be found in various major and minor keys, a major triad can be thought of as being a I, III, IV, V, or VI. This means that the C-major triad can be found diatonically in at least five keys, and can serve as an entry to any of them. It will, of course, assume a different function in each key:

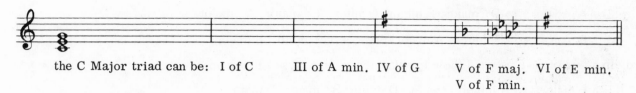

the C Major triad can be: I of C   III of A min. IV of G   V of F maj. VI of E min.
                                                                    V of F min.

Analyze and continue each of these sequential patterns based on **common-chord modulation**:

1.   I=IV

C: I   V   I   G: IV   I   ii6   V–7   I   etc.

2.   I=V

C: I   V   I   F: V V_5^6 I   ii6   V–7   I   etc.

b. Continue each of the following sequences until the original chord is reached again. Then repeat the pattern starting on the D- and E^b-major triads:

1.   I=VI

C: I   V7   I   E min.: VI   iv i_4^6 V   i   etc.

2.   I=III

C: I   V   I   A min.: III   VI $ii°_5^6$ V–7   i   etc.

c. In four-part block harmony, establish the given chord as the tonic of the key. (The simplest and quickest way to establish a key is by playing a I-V (or V^7) -I progression. Experiment with expansions of this progression, introducing other diatonic and chromatically altered chords into the progression before the final V-I.) Then use the given chord as the common chord with which to modulate into the keys that follow:

1.   D major: to A; B minor; F$^\sharp$ minor; G; D

2. A^b major: to D^b major; F minor; C minor; E^b major; A^b major

3. E major: to C$^\sharp$ minor; A major; B major; G$^\sharp$ minor; E major

d. In a free pianistic style, follow the plan above with these key schemes:

1. F major: to A minor; C major; D minor; B^b major; F major

2. B major: to G$^\sharp$ minor; E major; F$^\sharp$ major; D$^\sharp$ minor; B major

3. E^b major: to A^b major; G^b minor; B^b major; C minor; E^b major

e. A minor triad has the possibility of being considered as i, ii, iii, iv, or vi:

the D minor triad can be: i of D min.   ii of C Maj.   iii of B♭ Maj. iv of A min. vi of F Maj.

Resolve each of these minor triads to the four keys to which it belongs, other than its own tonic.

f. Continue the following sequences until the beginning triad is reached again:

Invent two sequential patterns in which the C-minor triad becomes iii and vi.

g. In four-part block harmony, use each of the given minor triads as the common chord through which to modulate to the keys that follow, first establishing the chord as the tonic of the given key:

1. B minor: to A major; F$^\sharp$ minor; C$^\sharp$ minor; D major; B minor

2. G minor: to B^b major; D minor; E^b major; F major; G minor

3. E minor: to B minor; D major; G major; C major; E minor

4. F$^\sharp$ minor: to E major; D major; C$^\sharp$ minor; A major; F$^\sharp$ minor

h. Start with a short melodic motive and spin it, in a free pianistic style, over the harmonies involved in these modulations, using the first minor triad in each series as the common chord:

1. A minor: to E minor; G major; F major; C major; A minor

2. F minor: to D^b major; A^b major; C minor; E^b major; F minor

3. C$^\sharp$ minor: to E major; G$^\sharp$ minor; B major; A major; C$^\sharp$ minor

i. Modulation can be made via an intermediate common chord. For example, the keys of C major and A^b major have no chords in common. The C-major triad, however, can be considered the V of F minor. The F-minor triad can then, in turn, be considered the vi of A^b, and the modulation effected:

Use an intermediate common chord to make the following modulations:

1. G major to E^b major

2. B^b major to D^b major

3. E major to F major

4. A major to C major

5. B^b major to B major

6. D major to B^b major

j. Work out the following chain of modulations, using any of the common-chord processes discussed thus far:

1. D major − B minor − G major − A^b major − B^b minor − F major − D major

2. E minor − C major − D^b (C$^\sharp$) major − E major − F major − A minor − E minor

3. A^b major − C minor − E^b major − G^b (F$^\sharp$) major − E minor − C major − D^b major − A^b major

k. Work out:

1. Four common-chord modulations that move from the given major keys to the keys of their dominants: F, A, D^b, and E.

2. Four common-chord modulations that move from the given minor keys to their relative majors: G, B, E^b, C$^\sharp$.

3. Four common-chord modulations that move from the given major keys to their relative minors: A^b, D, G, F$^\sharp$.

4. Four common-chord modulations that move from the given major keys to their subdominants: B^b, F$^\sharp$, E^b, A.

l. Sequential patterns offer many possibilities for modulation:

1. The circle of fifths, with each triad becoming a V^7, can be stopped at any point and a new tonic established:

Choose an arpeggiated right-hand pattern and move through the circle of fifths from E major to B^b major; from F major to E minor; from G major to F$^\sharp$ minor.

2. Some of the sequential patterns of seventh chords given in the previous chapter can also be used for modulation purposes. Stop the pattern at an appropriate place to make a cadence:

Use sequential patterns of seventh chords to modulate from G to B major; from G^b to B^b.

m. Review sequential patterns using circles of fifths or thirds from previous chapters and use them for modulatory purposes.

EXERCISE 2: Modulation by Means of a Common Tone

Dvořák: Slavonic Dance

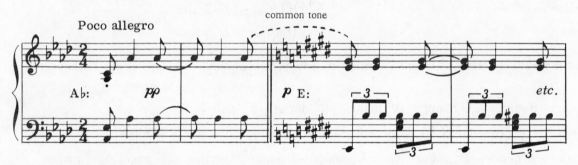

The delightful and surprising change of key in Dvořák's *Slavonic Dance*, illustrated above, is a clear example of the principle of modulating by means of a tone common to two keys. The tone A^b, which has been the tonic of a major scale, becomes, through an enharmonic change, the third of a new scale: E major. Essentially, modulation by means of a **common tone** (or tones) is based on the idea that a single tone has many scale relationships. The tone C, for example, can be 1 of C major and C minor, 2 of B^b major and minor, 3 of A^b major and A minor, 4 of G major and minor, etc.

a. Play a short phrase that establishes a key. Come to rest on a tone of that key and give that tone a scale function in a different key. The examples below show how this might be done:

b. Modulate by means of a common tone—which might be an enharmonic tone—from:

1. A^b major to D major
2. B minor to G minor
3. E^b major to A minor

4. F minor to D major
5. C$^\sharp$ major to B^b major
6. E major to F minor

c. It is interesting and instructive to make chains of common-tone modulations, as in this example:

d. In free pianistic style, modulate through the following series of keys, using the process of modulation by common tone:

1.   G minor — B major — E^b minor — D major — G minor

2.   C major — D minor — B major — A^b minor — E major — C major

3.   F minor — D major — G^b major — A major — F minor

4.   E major — C major — F$^\sharp$ minor — D minor — E major

e. The fact that a tone may be the root, third, fifth, seventh, or ninth (or thirteenth) of a major, minor, diminished, or augmented chord opens up a tremendous number of modulatory possibilities. Such modulation gives a gentle change of tonal center, as in this Brahms song where the D in the melody is in turn the root and the fifth of two seventh chords, and then the fifth and the ninth of chords from another tonality:

Brahms: "Es hing der Reif"

In the examples below, the tone C is used as the root, third, fifth, seventh, and ninth, with a resolution of a V^9 to a new tonality. In any measure after the first ones, a new key direction could have been followed:

After playing and analyzing the above examples, transpose them, using as the common tone: D, F, and A^b.

f. Use the technique of the above to effect these modulations: G to D; E^b to G^b; B^b to F; B minor to E minor; G minor to C minor.

g. Interesting shifts of key occur when a soprano or bass tone moves to its expected resolution—but an unexpected chord is substituted for the expected one:

Prokofiev: *Classical Symphony*

Improvise brief diatonic phrases, harmonizing the final melody tone in an unexpected fashion.

h. In the following examples, the bass of a V_2^4—which has a strong pull toward its I_6—resolves in

Nos. 2, 3, and 4 to its proper tone—but that tone becomes part of an unexpected chord:

i. Treat the following dominant sevenths in the manner illustrated in the preceding example:

j. Analyze the following sequential pattern and continue it until the starting chord is reached again:

etc.

EXERCISE 3: Modulation by Means of the Diminished Seventh Chord

The **diminished seventh chord** is most useful in modulation, since each of the three diminished seventh chords, by changing its spelling, can belong to four keys. Each diminished seventh chord thus can serve as a convenient harmonic intersection, or pivot:

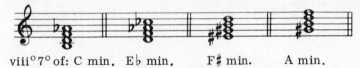

viii°7° of: C min.   Eb min.   F♯ min.   A min.

Play and analyze the following pattern. Repeat it, starting with the D minor triad, then with the E minor triad:

Lowering any tone of a diminished seventh chord allows that tone to become the root of a dominant seventh which could resolve to its major or minor tonic. (The same result can be achieved by holding one tone of the diminished seventh chord and raising the other three tones as in number 5.)

Utilizing this possibility allows for modulations such as:

Modulate, using the process shown above, from: C major to F# major; E minor to B♭ major; D major to A♭ major; C# minor to G minor.

EXERCISE 4: Melodic Modulation

Thus far, most of the examples and exercises have emphasized the use of harmony in modulation. It is possible to establish a key and move away from that key in purely melodic terms.

a. At the beginning of a new phrase, a different tone can be substituted for an expected one; the music now continues in the new key established by the unexpected tone, as in this example:

Choose a well-known folk tune and change the key of the melody at the beginning of each new phrase as shown above.

b. The same principle can be applied to such musical works as Hanon and Czerny exercises. Continue this melody which is based on a Hanon exercise. After several measures, reverse the motion and come down the scale, always changing key:

After Hanon

c. Spin a long, slow melodic line—a line that might be played by a clarinet—over a bass drum-beat; change the tonality of the melody every three or four measures. The example below shows the beginning of such a melody. Build it to a climax tone and then let it unwind:

Invent similar melodies, in a slow tempo and with constant key changes, that might be played by a 'cello, an oboe, a flute, and a tuba.

d. Continue the following scherzo-like melody and invent others over a fast drum-beat. Think of the melody as something written for piccolo or flute, and let it be full of unexpected tonal changes:

e. Abrupt shifts of tonality can occur when a melodic line hits a "surprise" tone—one that is completely unexpected. This tone forces a change, as though a rug were pulled out from under the original key. Analyze the example and improvise short lyrical pieces and dances in which similar sudden changes of tonality take place.

EXERCISE 5: The Uses of Modulation in Improvising and in Harmonizing Melodies

The term "modulation" is a multi-purpose word in music theory. There are modulations, as in a sonata or symphony, that lead to a new section in which a comparatively long time is spent in a key or keys other than the original one. There are other modulations that do not actually disturb the feeling for the original key, but provide tonal variety. Such modulations might be called "transient" or "pass-through" modulations.

a. Transient modulations moving through a series of tonalities are features of much nineteenth-century music. They are the result of harmonic sequences used for coloristic effects, as in this example where the key of C minor is not in question—the passage begins and ends in it:

Weber: *Der Freischütz*

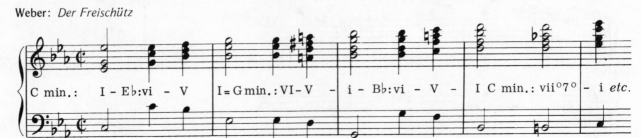

Play and analyze the Weber example above; then transpose it to the keys of D, E, and F minor.

b. Each of the following exercises contains at least one possible transient modulation effected by common tone (c.t.) or common chord (c.c.). Play each exercise, first in block harmony, then in a pianistic style:

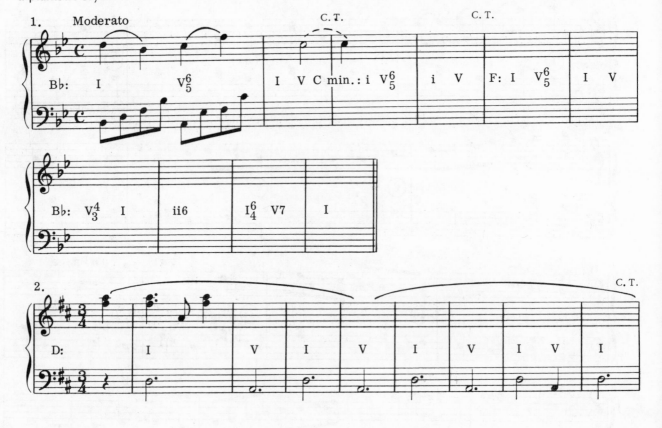

6. (a)

(b)

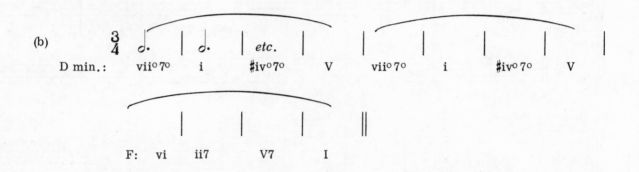

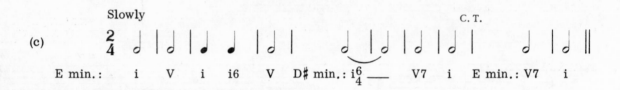

(c)

c. Find examples of transient modulations in the music of Chopin, Schubert, Schumann, et al. Analyze the modulations and improvise on them.

d. The Baroque dance forms, although short, usually contained one or more transient modulations. Harmonically, the first section established the tonic key, then modulated to the dominant or the relative major or minor key; the section closed with a cadence in the new key. The second part of the work was taken up by modulations that led back to the original tonic. The entire piece was usually based on the melodic material stated in the first two or four measures. Following are some short, complete, Baroque dance forms in harmonic outline. In a few instances, the starting measures are given and can be continued. First play block harmonies from the symbols; then convert the progressions into the dance forms:

1. Minuet

I^6_4 V E min.: V6 V____ V6 i V i D Maj.: ii V6 V V6

I IV6 IV IV6 B min.: V^4_3 V6____ i $ii°^4_3$ $ii°^6_5$ V $vii°^6_5$

$ii°^4_2$ V6 V7____ i VI6 $vii°_6$____ i6 iv V7 i____

2. Sarabande

2. Slowly

F Maj.: I vi I6 IV vii°6 V^6_5 I V V^4_2 I6 IV6 I^6_4 V

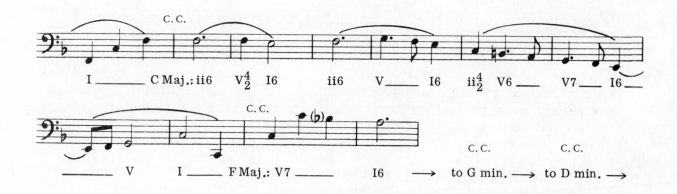

C. C.

I____ C Maj.: ii6 V^4_2 I6 ii6 V____ I6 ii^4_2 V6____ V7____ I6____

C. C.

____ V I____ F Maj.: V7____ I6 ⟶ to G min. ⟶ to D min. ⟶

C. C.   C. C.

to B♭ Maj. ⟶ to F Maj. ⟶ to Cadence.

3. Courante

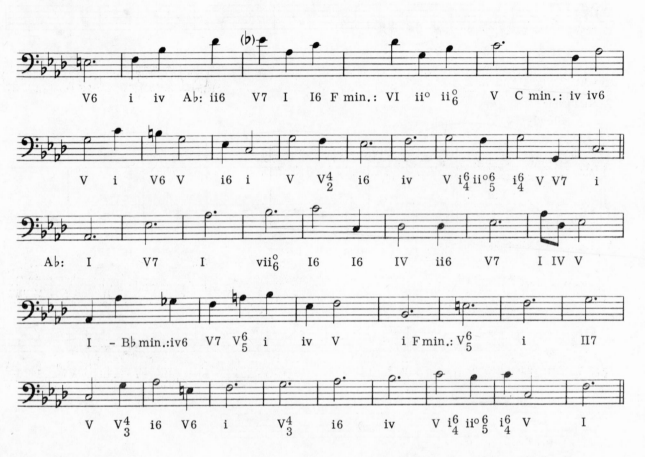

e. Select one of Bach's *Short Preludes* and write out its harmonic plan. Use that plan as the basis on which to improvise your own prelude. Try using the melodic material of one prelude over the harmonic plan of another.

f. Harmonize the following melodies, each of which includes one or more modulations, some of which are indicated:

1. Franz: "Waldfahrt"

2. Franz: "Wandl' ich in dem Wald des Abends"

G:

(E min.)

3. Franz: "Die Lotusblume"

G min.:

4. Franz: "Frühlings Ankunft"

5. "The God of Abraham Praise"

G min.:

6. Himmel: "Holy Ghost Dispel Our Sadness"

7. Chorale, "Erschienen ist der herrliche Tag"

8. Chorale, "Ach lieben Christen, seid getrost"

9. Schumann: "Lied der Braut (II)"

G: V7

A min.:

C:

G:

10. Franz: "Aus meinen grossen Schmerzen"

Andante

F:

11. A. Scarlatti: "O, cessate di piagarmi"

Fine

E min.:

B min.:

C:

D:

D. C.

G:

12. Purcell: "Fairest Isle"

18

CHROMATICISM: EXTENSIONS OF TRADITIONAL DIATONIC HARMONY

Augmented Sixth Chords; The Neapolitan Sixth; The Diminished Seventh as a Chromatic Chord; Other Forms of Chromaticism; The Ultimate in Chromaticism: Non-Tonal Music; Other Aspects of Contemporary Music

Chromaticism, the introduction into a musical work of tones outside the diatonic scale or tonality in which the work is based, is to be found in music of all periods. The nineteenth century is sometimes referred to as "the age of chromaticism," but the use of tones that are foreign to a key can be traced back at least as far as the middle ages. Chromaticism can be applied to music based on the modes as well as to music in a major or minor tonality.

While chromaticism may be present in a melody or in an harmonic progression, a chromatic melody need not call for a chromatic harmonization. Nor does a chromatic harmonic progression necessarily accompany a chromatic melody.

In the example below, No. 1 shows a chromatic melody over diatonic chords; No. 2 shows a diatonic melody harmonized with chromatic chords:

1. Saint-Saëns: *Samson and Delilah*

2. Gottschalk: *L'Union*

The varieties of chromaticism are almost limitless. Some chromatically altered chords became so common in musical usage, however, that they have been given names and, to some extent, functions. Chords in this category include the three types of augmented sixth chords and the Neapolitan sixth chord.

THE AUGMENTED SIXTH CHORDS

The **augmented sixth chords** are named for the interval of the augmented sixth which appears between the bass tone and one of the upper tones in the chord:

EXERCISE 1: The Italian Sixth

The **Italian sixth chord**, a triad, is the simplest and the basic augmented sixth chord. It usually occurs as the first inversion of a minor sub-dominant triad with a raised root:

Tartini: Sonata for Violin ("The Devil's Trill")

Note that the fifth of the triad, the tone that does not form part of the augmented sixth interval, is doubled. In major, the bass tone of the augmented sixth chords is the lowered sixth degree of the scale. In minor, it is the sixth degree which, in harmonic minor, is already lowered.

a. Practice building Italian sixths on the following bass notes. First find the augmented sixth interval (which feels like a minor seventh on the keyboard). Then add the fifth of the triad, which is the tone that lies a major third or tenth above the bass tone, as illustrated in No. 1:

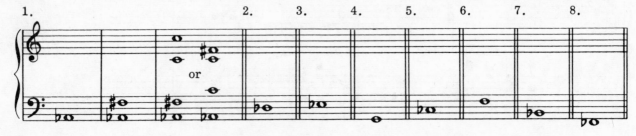

b. The Italian sixth, which can occur in major as well as in minor, usually functions as a pre-cadence chord, moving either to the dominant or to the tonic $\frac{6}{4}$:

c. Convert each of these sub-dominant triads into Italian sixths and resolve them:

d. Analyze, then transpose the following cadential phrase to the major keys of A^b, E, D, F$^\sharp$, B^b, and D^b:

e. The figured bass symbol for the Italian sixth is $\frac{6}{3}$ or $\frac{\sharp 6}{3}$. Realize the following figured basses; each uses one or more Italian sixths:

f. Harmonize the following melodic fragments, each of which contains at least one possible place to use an Italian sixth. Look for a first scale degree or a raised fourth scale degree as possible places to use it:

EXERCISE 2: The French Sixth

The **French sixth** is a chromatically altered form of the super-tonic seventh in second inversion:

Beethoven: *Piano Sonata, Opus 13*

a. The following tones represent the second degree of the scales indicated by the key signatures. Convert the diatonic seventh chords built on these tones to French sixths, as in No. 1:

1.   Play the super-tonic sevenths on the given bass tone.

2.   Put the chord in second inversion.

3.   In major, lower the bass tone and raise the third of the chord. In minor, raise the third of the chord.

4.   Resolve the resulting French sixth to a tonic $\frac{6}{4}$.

b. Analyze the following sequential patterns; then continue each one until the starting chord is reached again:

3.

etc.

c. Compose harmonic phrases that include at least one French sixth. Use each phrase as a basis for improvisations, exploring its melodic possibilities. The harmonic rhythm might be moderately fast or quite slow:

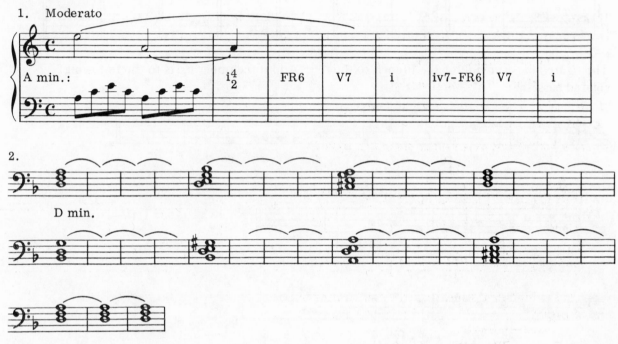

d. Each of the following brief melodies contains at least one place to use a French sixth. Harmonize each melody in chorale or free style:

e. If you prefer, think of the French sixth as an Italian sixth with an added tone: the note an augmented fourth above the bass. Practice building French sixths, thinking of them this way. First find the augmented sixth interval; add the tone a major third above the bass, to make the basic Italian sixth chord. Then fill in the added tone. (Note that the added tone is always a major second above the third.) Repeat the exercise, resolving each French sixth chord to a tonic $\frac{6}{4}$, and to a dominant seventh, as in No. 1 below:

f. The figured bass symbol for the French sixth is $\begin{smallmatrix}\sharp 6\\4\\3\end{smallmatrix}$. Add three upper parts to the following figured basses:

g. The V^7 with a lowered fifth used in second inversion:

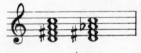

G: V7   ♭5V7

has the same interval structure as a French sixth, but resolves to the I or i, as in this sequential pattern. Continue the pattern until the starting chord is reached again:

h. The sound of the French sixth has intrigued composers, possibly because of its whole-tone scale implications:

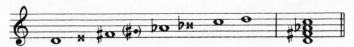

Analyze and develop the following:

1.

2.

3.

EXERCISE 3: The German Sixth

The following example shows an Italian sixth, a French sixth, and a **German sixth**:

a. Analyze the German sixth, and continue the above pattern through the circle of fifths.

b. The same German sixth, in sound, appears in two spellings: as a first inversion of a sub-dominant chord, as in No. 1 below; or as the second inversion of a super-tonic chord, as in No. 2 below:

The German sixth, like the French sixth, can be thought of as an Italian sixth with an added tone. Here the added tone is the note a perfect fifth above the bass. Build German sixths above the following bass tones. First find the interval of the augmented sixth; then add a major third and a perfect fifth above the bass. Play each chord in close position; then play it in several other spacings, as indicated:

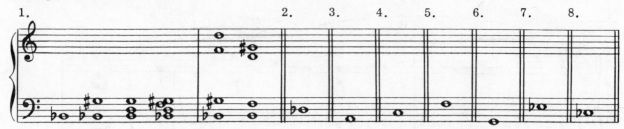

c. The German sixth, like other forms of augmented sixth chords, is most often found as a pre-cadential chord, as in this example:

Beethoven: Piano Sonata, Opus 13

d. Analyze the voice leading in the following examples:

Following the pattern of the above resolutions, resolve each of the following German sixths to a tonic $\frac{6}{4}$ followed by a dominant and a tonic; or, resolve them directly to a V or V^7:

e. Continue the following sequential patterns until the first chord is reached again. Then repeat the patterns, starting a half step lower:

f. Composers often use the German sixth in highly chromatic modulations, as in this example based on a phrase from Schubert's song, "Die Post." Continue the sequential pattern until the starting chord is reached again. Repeat the exercise, starting on a C-major triad:

Poco animato

g. A German sixth may occur as part of a long harmonic phrase, moving onward by step rather than resolving to the V or the I$_6^4$:

Analyze the above harmonic phrase and use it as the basis for several improvisations such as études, nocturnes, lyrical pieces, etc.

h. The German sixth sounds like a dominant seventh, and vice versa. Analyze the following example, and transpose it to the minor keys of G, B, E, F♯, and E♭:

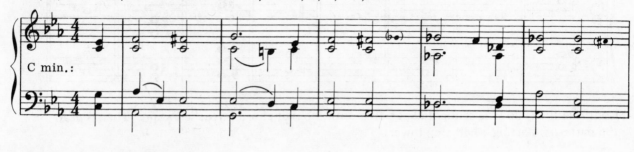

C min.:

Improvise phrases in which dominant sevenths become German sixths, or German sixths become dominant sevenths.

i. The German sixth is useful at cadence points, particularly in harmonizing scale degrees 1, ♭3, and ♯4. Harmonize the melodic fragments below. Each of them has at least one place to use a German sixth:

1.

2.

3.

4.

j. Compose harmonic phrases that include German sixths and improvise on them.

THE NEAPOLITAN SIXTH

The **Neapolitan sixth** (N6) is a major triad built on the lowered second degree of a major or minor scale. It is used principally in its first inversion:

Schubert: "Der Müller und der Bach"

The chord was given its name because its dramatic quality was first exploited by Neapolitan opera composers who used it as a pre-cadential chord which progressed to a dominant or a tonic $^6_4$. (Some theorists account for the Neapolitan sixth chord as a borrowing from the Phrygian mode.)

EXERCISE 4: The Neapolitan Sixth

a. Play the following exercise in the major keys of A^b, D, and G, and in the minor keys of C, F$^\sharp$, and B:

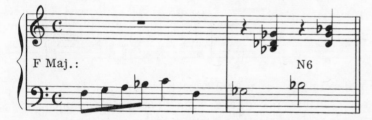

b. Build N6 chords on the following bass tones and resolve them. Think of each bass tone as the third of a major triad; the root of the N6 will be a half step above the tonic of the scale.

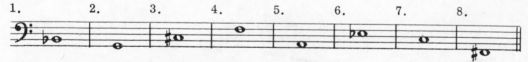

c. Play the following examples of the N6 in C minor. Analyze the voice leading and doubling. Transpose the examples to the minor keys of G, F, B, F$^\sharp$, and E^b:

d. Continue the following sequential patterns until the starting chord is reached again:

1. The tonic tone of the original scale becomes the bass of a N6 in the new key:

2. A major tonic chord in first inversion becomes a N6 that resolves to a new tonic; each new phrase begins a whole tone higher than the previous one:

e. Play and analyze each of the following musical examples. Then reduce each to block harmony and transpose the harmonic progressions to at least three other keys. Finally, use the harmonic progressions as bases for several improvisations in styles different from the originals. (Note that in the third example the N6 appears as a triad in *root* position.)

1. Mozart: Quintet in G minor, K. 516

Allegro

2. Grieg: *Notturno*

3. Grieg: *Volksweise*

f. The figured bass symbol for the N6 in minor is $^{\flat 6}_{\ 3}$; in major it is $^{\flat 6}_{\flat 3}$. Realize the following figured

basses. Note that in some cases the N6 progresses to a chord other than a V or a I$_6^4$:

4.

g. The chord numerals for the N6 are ^{b}II$_6$. Improvise on the following chord patterns that use N6's:

1.   A minor: Andante   i-iv | $^\#$iv-V^7 | i-i$_6$ | V$_6$-i | ^{b}II$_6$-V^7 | i$_6$-^{b}II$_6$ | i$_6$-V^7 | i ‖
                  12/8   5

2.   D minor: Largo   i-i$_4$-ii°^{7}-V^7 | i-i$_4$-ii°^{7}-V^7 | i-VI-^{b}II$_6$ | V$_4$-V^7 | i ‖
                  4/4   2   2   3

3.   G major: Andante   I-V$_4$ | I$_6$-IV$_6$ | I$_6$-^{b}II$_6$ | vii°$_4$-I$_6$ | ii-I$_6$ | ii$_6$-V^7 | I ‖
                  3/4   2   4   3   5

h. Use at least one N6 in each of the following modulations:

1.   From G minor to D^b major

2.   From E major to E^b minor

3.   From C$^\#$ minor to C major

i. Harmonize the following short melodies, using at least one N6 in each harmonization:

1.

2.

3.

EXERCISE 5: Harmonization of Long Melodies Using Augmented and Neapolitan Sixth Chords

Each of the following melodies has at least one place to use an augmented sixth or a Neapolitan sixth chord. Not all the melodies are complete; some end in a key other than the starting key. First harmonize each melody with block chords. Then improvise a pianistic accompaniment that seems appropriate:

1. Chopin: Mazurka, Opus 30, No. 2

2. Barnaby: "Jesus, Where'ere Thy People Meet"

3. Kennedy: "Say Au Revoir but Not Good-Bye"

4. Bellini: *Norma*

5. Mozart: *The Abduction from the Seraglio*

Andante

Ger6   VI

6. Schumann: "Und wüssten's die Blumen"

7. Schumann: "Hör ich das Liedchen klingen"

Langsam

(C min.)

8. Dykes: "One There Is Above All Others"

III7 IV   Fr6

C min.: It6   Ab: Db:

Ab: #iv°7°

9. Wolf: "Die ihr schwebet"

C: It6   E min.: I$_4^6$ V E Maj.: It6

$^\sharp_\sharp{}^6_4$ $^\sharp_\sharp{}^5_3$ Ab Maj.:

10. Schubert

III7

EXERCISE 6: Improvisation on Long Harmonic Phrases

Each of the following chord patterns has at least one augmented sixth or Neapolitan sixth in it.
Play each pattern in block chords. Then use the pattern as the basis for an improvisation that
might be a song, a dance form, a prelude built on a motive, etc.:

a. A major: Allegro I-I$_6$-I | IV-VI$_4^3$-ii | ii-ii$_6$-II$_4^3$ | V-^{b}5II$_4^3$-III | V$_4^3$-V-V$_4^2$ | I$_6$-ii$_6$-V$^7_5$ | I ‖
9/8

b. E^b major: Animato I | V-I | V-I | V-I^{b7} | IV^{b7} | ^{b}VII | ^{b}VII | II$_4^3$ | $^\sharp$iv$^\sharp{}^6_{b5}{}_3$ | I$_6$ | I$_6$ | I$_6$-VI$_4^2$ | V^7 | V^7 | I | I ‖
6/8

c. G minor: Andante i-$^\sharp$iv$^\sharp{}^6_{b5}{}_3$ | V-i$_6$ | ii$_6$-V^7 | i | i-V^7 | i$_6$-i | i-V^7 | i-V^7 | i-i$_6$ | iv-V^7 | VI-I$_6^5$ | ^{b}II$_6$-i$_6^4$-V^7 | i ‖
6/8

d. F minor: Andante i | ii$_6$-V^7 | i | III^{b7} | VI i$_6^4$ | V^7 | i-ii$_6$-III$_6^5$ | ^{b}II$_6$ | ^{b}II$_6^4$ | VI | i$_6$-i$_6$-i | ii$_6$-V^7 | i |
3/4

vii^{o7o} | I ‖

e. B major: Andantino I | vi | ii$_6$ | V^7 | I-III | vi | III$_6^4$ | V^7 | I | VI^7 | ii-^{b}5II$_4^3$ | V^7 | I-III | vi | III$_6^4$ | V^7 | I ‖
2/4

f. D minor: Slowly
2/4
$$i\text{-}V \mid VI\text{-}ii_6 \mid i_6\text{-}V \mid i\text{-}i_6 \mid iv\text{-}I_4 \mid iv_6\text{-}{}^{b}II_6 \mid i_6\text{-}V^7 \mid VI\text{-}ii_6 \mid i_6\text{-}V^7 \mid i_6\text{-}ii_6 \mid i_6\text{-}{}^{\#}iv \, {}^{\#}{}^{6}_{b5} \mid$$

$$i_6 \mid V^7 \mid i \mid i \mid$$

THE DIMINISHED SEVENTH AS A CHROMATIC CHORD

The diminished seventh chord is one of the most useful chromatic harmonies. It has been used poignantly by Bach, brilliantly by Chopin and Liszt, dramatically menacingly by Weber and Verdi, and yearningly by Schumann. In a more humble role, it was an important element in the barber-shop harmonies used by composers of sentimental popular songs of the 1890's.

EXERCISE 7: Harmonic Progressions and Improvisations Using the Diminished Seventh as a Chromatic Chord

a. Practice harmonizing the ascending and descending chromatic scale, alternating diminished sevenths and triads, as in the examples below. Continue each example:

b. Any chord of a major or minor scale can be preceded by the diminished seventh chord whose root lies a half step below the diatonic chord's root. The following examples show how this is done in the key of C major. After playing and analyzing the examples, transpose them to the keys of B minor, F minor, A major, and E^b major:

Improvise musical ideas based on the exercises above. The following example shows one possibility:

Ped. PT.

c. The following exercises should be continued, to complete the embellishment of the descending C-major scale. Repeat the exercises in the keys of A minor, G minor, E major, and B^b major:

1.

vii°7°_____ I   #vi°7°___ vii   #v°7°_____ vi

2.

vii°7°_____ I   #vi°7°

d. In this exercise, each diatonic chord of the ascending major scale is preceded by its embellishing diminished seventh. Complete the scale of C; then repeat the exercise in the keys of D minor, F$^\sharp$ minor, A^b major, and B major:

vii°7°_____ I   #i°7°_____ ii   #ii°7° etc.

e. Continue this Schumannesque sequence through the ascending scale of G major. Then transpose the exercise to the keys of C minor, E minor, D major, and F major:

f. Nineteenth-century composers used series of diminished seventh chords for bravura or dramatic effects, as in Chopin's Etude, Op. 10, No. 3:

1.

2.

Improvise other bits of passage-work based on diminished sevenths.

Basing an improvisation on an already existing motive or theme can be both interesting and instructive. Since, in this process, there is no need to strive for originality of theme, the improviser can concentrate on the manipulation of the musical material. The search for "originality" too often leads to a self-consciousness that hinders rather than helps. Most music—even the greatest—grows out of the residue of a composer's musical experience.

g. Improvise short pieces based on melodic material growing out of the diminished seventh chord. The following fragments should be continued for about twenty measures. (The first example is based on the opening of Bach's Suite for Solo 'Cello in D minor.)

1. Slowly

2. Fast

h. The diminished seventh has been used by many composers for its dramatic effect. Continue the fragment below, in which the diminished seventh is used as the harmonic basis of a recitative-like contrast to the full block harmonies of the opening:

Deliberately

Improvise other dramatic uses of the diminished seventh, being sure to test its effects in all registers.

i. Interesting harmonic sounds result from the use of consecutive diminished sevenths, with accented non-harmonic tones, as in this example. Extend the example for twelve to twenty more measures:

Slowly

EXERCISE 8: Using the Diminished Seventh Chord to Harmonize Melodies

a. The diminished seventh can be used to harmonize lower neighboring tones, as in the example below. Transpose the example to the keys of A, B, E^b, D^b, and G^b:

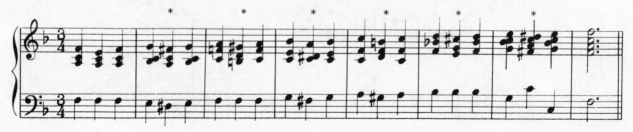

b. The diminished seventh chord can also be used to harmonize chromatic passing tones, or to embellish diatonic tones, as in this harmonization of "Sweet Genevieve," a melody that includes both chromatic passing tones and chromatic neighboring tones:

Harmonize the following brief melodies, each of which contains at least one place to use an embellishing diminished seventh:

c. An embellishing diminished seventh is often used to replace the repetition of a tonic chord, particularly in harmonizing sentimental songs. Note that the melody remains diatonic:

Harmonize the following short melodies, each of which contains at least one place to use an embellishing diminished seventh to replace a repeated diatonic chord:

d. Embellishing diminished seventh chords are basic to "close" or "barber-shop" harmony. They are especially useful in moving from one position of a V^7 to another:

Analyze the following sequential pattern and continue it through the circle of fifths until the first chord is reached again. Then work out the pattern with these melodies: 2-#2-3-4; 4-#4-5-5; 5-6-6-7:

Improvise phrases using embellishing diminished seventh chords. Be sure to explore spacing, use of different registers, and textures.

e. Diatonic chords can be converted into diminished seventh chords to intensify the harmony at cadence points, as in this chorale harmonization. Play the example first without the chromatic tones; then play it again, including them:

Play the melodic series 3-2-1-1-7-1 in the keys of B^b, E, A, and G^b major, harmonizing the series as Bach did in the example above.

f. Mozart was especially fond of using an embellishing $^\sharp$iv^{o7o} to intensify a cadence:

1. Piano Sonata, K. 280   2. Piano Sonata, K. 545

Harmonize the following melodic series, following the pattern of the Mozart excerpts:

1.   In the minor keys of G, A, E, and C: 8-8-3-4-2-1; 1-8-5-4-2-1; 1-3-3-2-4-3.

2.   In the major keys of E^b, F$^\sharp$, B, and C$^\sharp$: 6-7-8-1; 8-7-6-5; 4-2-1-3.

g. A chromatic diminished seventh has been used by composers to intercept a cadential resolution, thereby extending an harmonic phrase:

Mozart: Piano Sonata, K. 310

Improvise phrases that avoid final cadences by substituting a chromatic diminished seventh for the expected chord of resolution.

h. Harmonize the following melodies, each of which has at least one place to use an embellishing diminished seventh. In a few instances an asterisk (*) is used to indicate a possible place to use a diminished seventh:

1. **Gottschalk:** *The Last Hope*

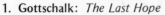

2. **Calkin:** "Fling Out the Banner"

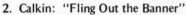

3. **Tucker:** "Sweet Genevieve"

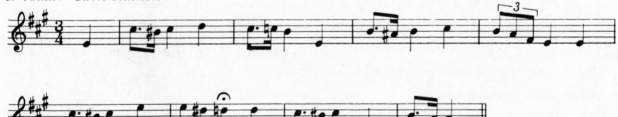

4. **Wolf:** "Verborgenheit"

Slowly

vi–Aug6   I⁶₄

EXERCISE 9: Improvising with the Diminished Seventh Chord in Long Harmonic Patterns

Each of the following long harmonic patterns contains at least one embellishing diminished seventh. Play the patterns first in block chords; then improvise on each pattern, trying several styles:

a. A major: Allegro Moderato
                9/8

$$\text{I-I}_6\text{-I} \mid \text{IV-VI}_{4\atop 3}\text{-ii} \mid\mid \text{ii-ii}_6\text{-II}_6 \mid \text{V-}^\flat 5\text{VII}_{4\atop 3}\text{-III} \mid \text{V}_4\text{-V-V}_{4\atop 2} \mid \text{I}_6\text{-I-I} \mid\mid$$

$$^\sharp\text{I}^\circ{}_{6\atop\natural 5}\text{-II-}\,^\sharp\text{I}^{\circ 7\circ} \mid \text{ii-ii}_6\text{-ii} \mid \text{vii}_{4\atop 3}\text{-I}_6\text{-V}_6 \mid \text{I-vii}_6\text{-I}_6 \mid \text{II}_{6\atop 5} \mid \text{II}_{6\atop 5} \mid \,^\sharp\text{iv}^{\circ 7\circ} \mid$$

$$^\sharp\text{iv}^\circ{}_{6\atop\natural 5} \mid \text{I}_6 \mid \text{V}^7 \mid \text{I}_6\text{-ii}_6\text{-V} \mid \text{I} \mid\mid$$

b. D minor: Moderato
                2/2

$$\text{i} \mid \text{VI}_6 \mid \text{vii}^\circ{}_{6\atop 5} \mid \text{i}_6 \mid \,^\sharp\text{iii}^{\circ 7\circ} \mid \text{iv} \mid ^\flat\text{VII}^7 \mid \text{III}_6\text{-III} \mid ^\flat\text{VII-vii}^{\circ 7\circ} \mid \text{i-V}_{4\atop 3}\text{-i} \mid$$

$$\text{V} \,^\sharp\text{iv}^{\circ 7\circ} \mid \text{i}_6\text{-V}^7\atop 4 \mid \text{i} \mid\mid$$

c. C minor: Lightly
                3/8

$$\text{i} \mid \text{V}_{4\atop 3} \mid \text{i}_6 \mid \text{I}_{6\atop 5} \mid \text{iv} \mid \text{i}_{6\atop 4} \mid \,^\sharp\text{iv}^\circ \,^\sharp{}_{6\atop 5} \mid \,^\sharp\text{iv}^\circ \,^\sharp{}_6 \mid \text{V}_6 \mid \text{V}_6 \mid \text{i} \mid \text{VI} \mid \text{ii}_{6\atop 5} \mid \text{V}^7 \mid \text{i} \mid\mid$$

In the nineteenth century, as musical forms expanded in length, harmonic rhythms also became slower. The resources of chromaticism may have contributed to the process, allowing a composer to dwell on an harmonic sound which could be embellished to provide interest over the lengthened duration. The example below shows a dominant seventh built on G which lasts for four measures and is decorated with multiple neighboring tones that form diminished sevenths. At measure 5, the bass slides down a half step to F$^\sharp$, which becomes the root of a new dominant:

Continue the example above for several phrases. Then improvise other musical ideas which utilize the principle of prolongation through chromatic embellishment.

OTHER FORMS OF CHROMATICISM

While much chromaticism is simply the alteration of diatonic chords which continue to progress as though they were still diatonic chords, a great deal of chromaticism is the result of voice leading, with the melodic direction of the individual melodic lines determining chord progression. Such melodic movement often leads to unusual and dramatic harmonic progressions, as in the Gesualdo madrigal, "More lasso":

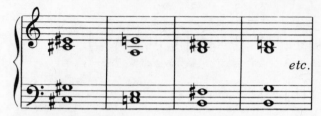

or in Bach's harmonization of a phrase of the chorale tune "Es ist genug" (quoted by Berg in his Violin Concerto):

Harmonic progressions such as those quoted above cannot be formularized. As voices move chromatically, they make their own logic. The varieties of chromaticism are almost limitless. The exercises that follow merely indicate some of the possibilities.

EXERCISE 10: The Augmented Tonic and Dominant

The augmented tonic (I+) and the augmented dominant (V+) are common chromatic chords, usually resulting from the raising of the fifth of the chord by a half step:

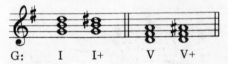

The upward motion of the half step creates a tendency toward another half-step motion:

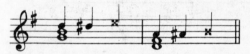

The resolution tone—E or B in the example below—can become the root, third, or seventh of a chord:

a. Transpose the example above to the keys of E^b, $F^\sharp$, A^b, and B.

b. Improvise an harmonic phrase that establishes a tonality; add two or three more phrases that use the I+ and the V+. Use the harmonic pattern as a basis on which to improvise a sentimental song, a march, and a waltz.

EXERCISE 11: Sliding Chromaticism

Sliding chromaticism is based on the movement of individual voices by half step. Start with a triad (C major, for instance); move one voice at a time and listen to the interesting sounds that result from the melodic movement. The example below, which should be continued, shows the principle in a simple form:

a. Melodic/harmonic progressions should always have a sense of direction. Following are a series of starting chords and their destinations, with the movement between them to be worked out as in the example above. For variety, the motion can be changed so that a voice occasionally moves upward by a half step:

b. The half-step sliding chromatic was a favorite harmonic device of Chopin:

Prelude

c. Improvise melodic lines, using many long notes, over a descending harmonic pattern that moves one voice at a time in half steps:

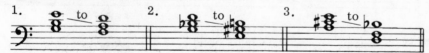

d. Sliding chromatics do not always have to move downward. Apply the principle of the Chopin Prelude moving upward, and improvise melodic lines over harmonies that move from:

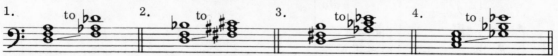

e. Sliding chromaticism is particularly useful to organists whose legatos are made only by the fingers, without the pianists' aid of the sustaining pedal:

Franck: Organ Chorale No. 3

Improvise patterns of upward- and downward-moving sliding chromaticism to fill in the harmonic progressions given below. Use finger legato only to move from the given starting chord to its destination:

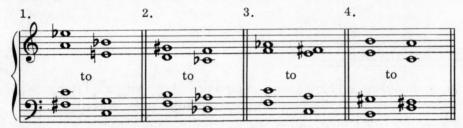

f. Sliding chromaticism can be combined with diatonic progressions, as in these harmonic phrases from Mozart and Granados. Note that the Granados also uses enharmonic changes. Play and analyze these progressions; then repeat each several times, starting a half step higher each time:

1. Mozart: Minuetto, K. 355

2. Granados: *Goyescas*, No. 1, "Los Requiebos" (harmonic outline)

Improvise new melodic lines and accompaniment patterns based on the Granados and Mozart harmonic progressions. Try various meters, textures, and registers. This fragment shows one possibility, based on the Granados:

g. Taking an harmonic phrase by a well-known composer and improvising new material based on it is an excellent way to get a feeling for different kinds of chromatic harmony and its possible uses. Play and analyze the following examples. Repeat them starting on other pitches. Then improvise freely on them.

1. Chopin: Mazurka, Opus 6, No. 1

2. Chopin: Mazurka, Opus 30, No. 4

h. The example given below illustrates the principle of sliding chromaticism in the bass. Inventing a strong bass, one that has a sense of direction, is a way of preventing chromatic music from floundering or seemingly getting nowhere:

Schubert: "Der Wegweiser"

Improvise freely on the Schubert pattern above. One possible improvisation based on this progression might start in this way:

Allegro moderato

i. The chromatic scale is, of course, the basic example of sliding chromaticism. Interesting harmonic sounds may be made by a bass line that moves in contrary motion against a chromatic scale in the upper voice. Continue each of the following examples up or down the chromatic scale to the indicated goal:

Note that when the chromatic scale is descending in the upper voice and the bass is moving in contrary motion, there will come a point at which the left-hand part will have to jump down an octave or two.

j. Here are two figured basses which should be fun to work out:

1. Schumann

k. Try improvising with the following chord progressions as a basis:

l. Chromaticism can be applied to the harmonization of major and minor, as well as chromatic scales, as in Bach's harmonization of a phrase of the chorale "Wie schön leuchtet der Morgenstern," which descends the E-major scale:

Scale harmonizations may involve chromatic triads, seventh, or ninth chords, as shown in these examples of harmonizations of the descending C-major scale:

Interesting harmonic sounds can also result from making the scale tones members of complex chordal combinations moving through a circle of fifths:

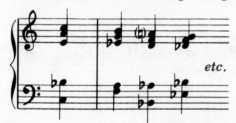

Invent at least six ways of harmonizing ascending and descending scales, using chromatics and various types of chords.

m. Experiment with the principle that chromatic melodic movement can result in unpredictable harmonic progressions:

Start with single tones and let voices move out from those tones:

1. After Moussorgsky
2.

Start with two intervals and move out or in from them:

Start with a seventh chord and use sliding chromatics:

THE ULTIMATE IN CHROMATICISM: NON-TONAL MUSIC

Intense chromaticism leads ultimately to a loss of tonality but opens up new harmonic and melodic possibilities.

EXERCISE 12: Improvising Non-Tonal Music

Make and write an arrangement of the twelve tones of the chromatic scale so that they do not suggest a major, minor, or modal scale. Here is one devised by a former student:

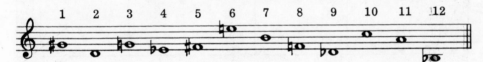

Use your arrangement as the basis for improvisations and exercises:

a. Improvise melodic lines that follow the order of tones in the arrangement, giving the arrangement rhythmic interest. Repeat the arrangement of tones several times, but in such a way that phrases do not always end on the twelfth tone, but rather, overlap, as in these examples:

Note that the melodic fragments given above make use of octave displacement, that is, writing or playing a tone an octave or more above or below its original register.

b. Make a long melodic line from the arrangement, and harmonize each tone with a traditional triad, seventh, or ninth chord:

c. Divide the tones of the arrangement between the hands, making a contrapuntal duet:

d. Play the arrangement from back to front, that is, in retrograde motion.

e. In this sequence of tones, improvise an additive melody, one in which a few tones are stated, repeated, and added to, etc.:

f. Make an accompaniment in which each of the twelve tones serves as the root of a major or minor triad. Then improvise melodies over the accompaniment:

g. Unusual, as well as usual, chords can be made by combining from three to six consecutive tones of the arrangement. Experiment with various spacings of the chords, as shown here:

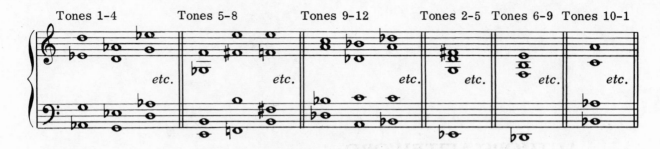

OTHER ASPECTS OF CONTEMPORARY MUSIC

Composing with the twelve tones in a non-tonal way—sometimes referred to as serial or dodecaphonic music—was developed and systematized by Arnold Schoenberg and his followers, Alban Berg and Anton von Webern. It can best be studied by examining the music written by these men, although other composers, such as Copland, Stravinsky, Dallapiccola, and Riegger, incorporated some aspects of twelve-tone writing into their techniques.

Twentieth-century composers have also explored and devised other technical resources. Intervals of seconds, fourths, and sevenths have been made the bases of harmonic sounds, ending the long hegemony of thirds and sixths. Two or more scales have been combined to produce the sound of polytonality, and triads have been superimposed to make polychords. Composers have invented new ways to use traditional triads, old modal scales, and medieval parallelism. Melodic and rhythmic practices of other cultures, including so-called "primitive" cultures, have been blended with Western European practices. Music has become randomly inspired, as well as totally controlled. Electronically generated sounds have become not only acceptable, but fashionable. And composers, notably Henry Cowell and John Cage, have treated the piano as a true percussion instrument, playing directly on the strings and the case, and even modifying the sounds of the strings themselves.

Many of the problems set forth in the first two parts of this book relate directly to twentieth-century practices, and the student might review them in the light of his added experience. The possible solutions of a musical problem are usually so numerous that the same problem can be worked on again and again without duplicating solutions. The student might also see how many types of percussive sounds he can make on, in, and under a piano.

AUTHORS' AFTERWORD

We hope that this book has given the student an insight into the creative process of learning, as well as equipping him with certain practical and technical skills. We also hope that he has developed courage to try things at the piano—outrageous as well as conventional—and that he has discovered the educative value of saying to himself: "I wonder what will happen if I . . . . "

RUTH AND NORMAN LLOYD